GRANDEUR PRESERVED

THE HOUSE MUSEUMS OF
HISTORIC CHARLESTON FOUNDATION

GRANDEUR 🌴 PRESERVED

HISTORIC CHARLESTON FOUNDATION

Introduction by Katharine S. Robinson
EXECUTIVE DIRECTOR

Charleston London

THE
History
PRESS

Published by The History Press
Charleston, SC 29403
www.historypress.net

All photography by Rick C. McKee unless otherwise noted.

Cover and design by Marshall Hudson

First published 2008

Manufactured in the United States

ISBN 978.1.59629.585.8

Grandeur preserved : the house museums of Historic Charleston Foundation / Historic Charleston Foundation.
p. cm.
Includes bibliographical references.
ISBN 978-1-59629-585-8
1. Historic buildings--South Carolina--Charleston. 2. Dwellings--South Carolina--Charleston. 3. Historic house museums--South Carolina--Charleston. 4. Historic buildings--South
Carolina--Charleston--Pictorial works. 5. Dwellings--South Carolina--Charleston--Pictorial works. 6. Historic buildings--Conservation and restoration--South Carolina--Charleston.
7. Dwellings--Conservation and restoration--South Carolina--Charleston. 8. Architecture, Domestic--Conservation and restoration--South Carolina--Charleston. 9. Charleston (S.C.)--
Buildings, structures, etc. 10. Charleston (S.C.)--Buildings, structures, etc.--Pictorial works. I. Historic Charleston Foundation (Charleston, S.C.)
F279.C48A2 2008
975.7'91503--dc22
2008037226

Historic Charleston Foundation is dedicated to preserving and protecting the historical, architectural and cultural character of Charleston and its historic environs, and to educating the public about Charleston's history and the benefits that are derived from preservation.

Nathaniel Russell House Committee Chairs (1955–2008)
Henry P. Staats
Mrs. John P. Frost
Mrs. J. Blake Middleton
Mrs. R.N.S. Whitelaw
Mrs. William O. Hanahan
Douglas B. Lee
Thomas R. Bennett
Virginia Dawson Lane

Aiken-Rhett House Committee Chairs (1996–2008)
Robert N. Rosen
Susan T. Friberg
Dwayne M. Green

CONTENTS

ACKNOWLEDGMENTS

The preservation and interpretation of Historic Charleston Foundation's historic house museums encompass many disciplines and are highly successful because of the research and ongoing stewardship of professional staff, consultants, and Foundation trustees and committee members. Their combined expertise has contributed enormously to the publication of this book and for that we are eternally grateful.

Very special thanks go to the following for their unparalleled support of Historic Charleston Foundation and particularly for their essential and integral involvement in every aspect of the museum houses and ultimately this publication:

Fielding S. Freed, Director of Museums

Valerie K. Perry, Associate Director

Brandy S. Culp, Curator

Carrie E. Naas, Aiken-Rhett House Manager

Judith H. Middleton, Museum Administrator

Jennifer M. Mortensen, Preservation Department

Minh V. Nguyen, Maintenance Department

Susan L. Buck, PhD

William J. Graham

Mr. and Mrs. Henry Hutson

William Elliott Hutson II

Mary Pope Maybank Hutson

Glenn F. Keyes

Robert A. Leath

Patricia Loughridge

Carl R. Lounsbury, PhD

Richard D. Marks III

Rick C. McKee

Jonathan H. Poston

Orlando Ridout V

J. Thomas Savage Jr.

Christine Thomson

Martha A. Zierden

INTRODUCTION

Charleston is one of the most important historic cities in North America. Its remarkable level of preservation has made it a premier cultural heritage site. Historic Charleston Foundation plays a central role in that regard and, in addition, interprets the city's history through the Foundation's two stellar museum houses. As one explores the Lowcountry, and particularly the historic sites that are open to the public, it is clear that the Nathaniel Russell and Aiken-Rhett properties are key landmarks and vastly important interpretive venues. The Foundation's two houses and the artifacts within them poignantly illustrate the integral connections between the past and the present and relate the social history of the people who lived and worked therein.

This publication sets forth, for the first time, a comprehensive retrospective of two of America's most stunning museum houses. The trustees and staff of Historic Charleston Foundation understand and appreciate their role as stewards of these vastly important properties and present to you, the reader, a thoroughly detailed and documented study of these magnificent properties through text and images.

The operation of our two museum houses is a dynamic and most important endeavor for Historic Charleston Foundation. Foundation staff members continuously research the genealogy of the Russell and Aiken-Rhett families and their household inventories, which in turn provide information about their collections and give appropriate direction for the accession of new items. New acquisitions create exciting interpretive opportunities for the museum house docents to share with the public the Foundation's remarkable collection of decorative and fine arts while promoting interest in Charleston's architectural, cultural, and social environment. The preservation of these magnificent properties extends beyond their physical restoration and conservation to include our efforts to protect our invaluable collections and help define preservation in America for the twenty-first century.

Katharine S. Robinson
EXECUTIVE DIRECTOR
HISTORIC CHARLESTON FOUNDATION

**Nathaniel Russell House,
51 Meeting Street, circa 1808.**

The house's overall design is
reflective of London's neoclassical
town houses. Craftsmen,
including enslaved African
Americans, constructed the
Nathaniel Russell House using
locally made Carolina gray brick
with imported white marble
ornament.

THE NATHANIEL RUSSELL HOUSE, CIRCA 1808

51 Meeting Street

For two centuries, visitors have admired the grand Federal-style town house of prominent merchant Nathaniel Russell. Completed in 1808, when Russell was seventy years old, the lavishly ornamented house serves as a testament to the immense wealth that he accumulated over his distinguished lifetime. Historic Charleston Foundation operates the site as a house museum. The evolution of its history provides a window into the city's past while also demonstrating the Foundation's commitment to preserving the Lowcountry's built and cultural environment.

Nathaniel Russell: "A Merchant of Great Wealth"

Throughout the eighteenth century, Charleston experienced exponential growth and ascending economic prosperity. As a result, the city attracted individuals in great numbers from other colonies and abroad who were eager to try their luck in search of financial gain. Nathaniel Russell was one such businessman.

Born in Bristol, Rhode Island, in 1738, Russell came to Charleston at the age of twenty-seven as an agent for Northern merchants. He quickly transitioned from factor to merchant and rose to a position of wealth and prominence in the community. Throughout his lifetime, he corresponded frequently with the most successful businessmen of his day, including Aaron Lopez and Nicholas Brown of Rhode Island and Elias Derby of Massachusetts.

Although Russell traveled frequently, maintaining his national and international connections, Charleston became his permanent home, but not without hesitation regarding the harsh Carolina summers. On July 19, 1767, Nathaniel Russell wrote to the Reverend Ezra Stiles of Newport, Rhode Island: "You will scarcely find one Comfortable Night in a month. I think there would be but very Little inducement to Tarry here was it not for the agreeable winters Together with the Kindness and Hospitality of the People."[1]

PORTRAIT OF NATHANIEL RUSSELL, **Boston, circa 1787, by Edward Savage (American, 1761–1820). Oil on canvas. Historic Charleston Foundation purchase, 58.1.26.**

The second son of a wealthy and socially prominent mercantile family, Russell was born in Bristol, Rhode Island, and ventured to Charleston to make his fortune.

In the mid- to late eighteenth century, while agricultural cash crops were the major source of revenue, Charleston's wealth was greatly fueled by mercantile endeavors. With profits from the sale of imported goods and African slaves, factors like Russell would purchase rice, indigo, deerskins, naval stores, and other commodities to be exported on behalf of their correspondents or partners. In this complex system of credit and exchange, Russell facilitated the trade of goods and acted as a factor, merchant, broker, and banker. Russell imported products such as English textiles, Rhode Island rum, and other commodities manufactured in the Northeast. He then brokered the purchase of agricultural goods from Lowcountry plantations and arranged the shipment of those commodities to both American and foreign ports of call, including Africa, Asia, England, France, Germany, and Russia.

Nathaniel Russell, like many Charleston factors and merchants, engaged in the slave trade. Partnering with merchants from the Northeast, predominantly Rhode Island, Russell arranged the import and sale of enslaved Africans. Russell noted on several occasions that he preferred to sell slaves who had recently arrived via the transatlantic passage, and he was shrewd to consistently advertise that his cargoes were "directly from Africa."[2] South Carolinians had a self-proclaimed prejudice against slaves imported from places other than the West African coast, which included individuals arriving via the Spanish

View of garden from second-floor balcony.

This garden is a twentieth-century interpretation of a nineteenth-century Charleston garden. In Russell's time, the garden would have featured a grouping of fancy grounds to the front with ornamental plants, trees, and shrubs. Locally famous botanist Philippe Noisette, who resided on Russell's Romney property, may have tended these gardens. Noisette advertised in 1814 that from his garden in Romney Village one could buy "a great Variety of FRUIT TREES, grafted by himself…such as different kinds of Peaches, Nectarines, Apricots, Plumbs, Pears, Apples, Figs, and Grapes; as well as many foreign, Ornamental Trees, Shrubs, and plants."

MINIATURE OF NATHANIEL RUSSELL, **Charleston, 1818, by Charles Fraser (1782–1860). Watercolor on ivory, inscribed: "Fraser/Painter" in the artist's hand, below in pencil, "Mr. Russell of Charleston/from life by C Fraser/Painter." Gift of Mrs. Henry Abbot, 92.5.3.**

Renowned Charleston artist Charles Fraser painted this miniature of Nathaniel Russell only two years before Russell's death. The entry for the commission is the first in Fraser's account book dated 1818 to 1839. Russell paid $50 for his miniature.

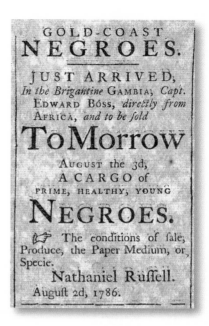

Slave trade advertisement, *CHARLESTON EVENING GAZETTE,* **August 2, 1786.**

Russell garnered a great deal of wealth from his dealings in the slave trade. He wrote to Aaron Lopez of Newport, Rhode Island, on July 14, 1772: "There has been a Great many negroes imported here this Summer & many more Expected. They continue at very Great Prices...If you should order a Cargo here Next Summer & favour [sic] me with the Sale of them, I make no Doubt but I should give you satisfaction." During the late eighteenth century, more ships sailed from Newport to Africa than from any other American port, and the majority of the Africans who endured the Middle Passage were brought to the Caribbean and Charleston. Russell facilitated such exchanges and made large profits for both himself and his associates in Rhode Island. *Courtesy of Charleston Library Society.*

colonies or through inter-colonial trade. As Russell explained to Newport merchant Aaron Lopez, it was difficult to sell slaves imported from other colonies, as they were "[g]enerally sent for some Capital Fault, which occasions the Purchasers to be very Cautious of Buying them."[3]

Russell enjoyed great economic success throughout the colonial era. When the Revolutionary War began, he lent more than £10,000 sterling to the Patriot cause and served in the Charleston militia in 1778 and in the third South Carolina General Assembly. Ultimately, he sided with the city's Tory merchants, and in the spring of 1780, he left the colonies for England during the invasion of Charleston. Neoclassicism was the height of fashion in Great Britain at that time, and the years Russell spent abroad would become greatly influential to the design and execution of the grand town house that he would build in Charleston almost three decades later.

A legislative ordinance in March of 1783 directed Russell's Charleston property confiscated, and when he returned to the city in September 1783, he was not allowed to disembark from his vessel. After petitioning the new legislature from aboard ship, he received a special exemption from the earlier ordinance and was able to return to his adopted city. Russell was one of the many Tories who repatriated and reestablished themselves in Charleston society.

In the years following the Revolutionary War, Russell continued his mercantile endeavors and invested heavily in Charleston real estate. He bought numerous town rental properties and plantation lands, including lot number 247 of the city's "Grand Modell," now known

Portrait of Alicia Russell (Mrs. Arthur Middleton), **Philadelphia, circa 1795–96, by Edward Savage (American, 1761–1820). Oil on canvas. Historic Charleston Foundation purchase, 67.1.1.**

Young Alicia Russell is shown picking roses, perhaps a reference to her family's love of gardening. Her mother and grandmother, both named Sarah Hopton, were among Charleston's most accomplished amateur gardeners. In 1818, William Faux, an English visitor to Charleston, remarked in *Memorable Days in America* that the Russells were "living in a nest of roses."

as 51 Meeting Street, which he acquired in 1779. At the time a series of working-class tenements stretched along the south side of the property, and in 1804 Russell advertised a "large and airy SCHOOL HOUSE, situated in *Price's Alley* near Meeting Street" for rent on the property.[4]

In 1788, at the age of fifty, Russell married the thirty-six-year-old Charleston heiress Sarah Hopton—a union that enhanced his standing in local society. Sarah was the daughter of William Hopton, a prominent colonial merchant. Their daughter, Alicia, was born the next year, followed by another daughter, Sarah, three years later. The growing family resided in a "3 story Brick House on the Bay" close to Russell's Cooper River wharves, where he could see the ships offloading onto the docks.[5]

Building the Russell House

Well established by the turn of the nineteenth century and with a family who would greatly benefit from a statelier abode, Russell made plans to construct a grand new residence on his Meeting Street property. At the age of seventy, his house would be his legacy, a testament to his wealth and an added assurance that his daughters would retain their place in Charleston society. His investments in commodities, land, and the slave trade had made him a wealthy man, and he spared no expense in the construction of the town house at 51 Meeting Street.

Inspired by Robert Adam's designs, the tripartite plan of Russell's house includes a rectangular, an elliptical, and a square room on each floor. A spacious reception room on the first floor is separated from the stair hall by glazed doors. The handsome cantilevered staircase rises three stories without any visible means of support, and the hall is lit by a large Palladian window on the lower flight and a recessed elliptical window on the upper flight. Carved wood, plaster, and applied composition ornament abound, reaching their apex in the second-story elliptical room. The house does not have the piazzas ubiquitous in Charleston architecture by this time, but instead boasts delicate wrought-iron balconies, the front embellished with Nathaniel Russell's initials. This balcony is referential to those on the façades of London's town houses of the mid- to late eighteenth century.

The architect of Russell's graceful neoclassical structure has not been discovered, and it has long been speculated that Russell either sketched his own plans or employed a local "gentleman amateur" to design the house. Regardless, the house is a reflection of the Russells' conception of refinement, and it is clear that Nathaniel Russell was greatly influenced by his travels to England thirty years prior. The contrasting surface values of the façade, use of balconies, tripartite geometrical plan, and ornament throughout harkens to the town house designs of prominent British architects of the late eighteenth and early nineteenth centuries. The elaborate cast plaster and composition ornament decorating the interior is an amalgamation of designs found in the published works of notable tastemakers, including Robert Adam, Placido Columbani, Batty and Thomas Langley, and William Pain. Classical motifs throughout the house, inspired by Roman and Greek art and architecture, make it one of the most notable neoclassical residential structures in America.

After completion, contemporaries considered the Russell House to be among Charleston's finest dwellings, and current perception has changed little over the past two hundred years. This grand building immediately attracted much admiration and attention. In 1811, only a few years after the house was built and lavishly furnished, tragedy struck the Russell family in the form of a tornado. The *Times* of Charleston reported extensively on the occurrence, noting that the "new large Mansion-House of Nathaniel Russell, esq. together with his extensive Back Buildings" were entirely unroofed and the windows broken, causing great damage. The *Charleston Courier* stated that Russell's "loss in, furniture, &c. cannot amount to less than $20,000."[6] Russell himself referred to his dwelling as "my Mansion House," and in his will, dated 1818, he stated the value of his property to be $38,000, which may have been a conservative reflection of the original cost.[7]

Front door and balcony.
Directly above the faux grain painted door, Nathaniel Russell's initials are prominently displayed in the cartouche of the handsome wrought-iron balcony.

An Accomplished Family

By the time he completed this house, Nathaniel Russell had become a prominent figure in Charleston, and he remained active in local organizations, even as an octogenarian. In 1819, he was elected president of the New England Society, a group of expatriate men from the Northeast. He had reached a most esteemed position among those in the community and afar. A visiting New England clergyman, Abiel Abbot, described Russell as "a merchant of great wealth & of greater benevolence, of high character and standing…against whom not a person in the city dares, if he could find the wish, to utter a syllable."[8]

While Russell was an important member of the community, his wife and two daughters were also known for their great accomplishments and charity. Nathaniel Russell signed a marriage agreement that allowed his wife Sarah to maintain control over the income, slaves, town rental properties, and plantation lands she brought into the marriage. As expected of an upper-class Charleston lady, Sarah was refined and well educated, and she and her husband ensured that both of their daughters were trained in the art of music as well as academic study. The girls were sent to New England to complete their education at Mrs. Newton's School in Medford, Massachusetts. Ann Newton was a sister of the famous American artist Gilbert Stuart, and her school was considered one of the most advanced for young women in the United States. She taught literature, mathematics, drawing, and needlework, and her advertisements emphasized the teaching of "manners and morals."

Alicia Russell was known by her contemporaries as a young lady of much grace and intelligence. In a letter dated August 1802, Nathaniel Bowen of Providence wrote to inform his sister Susan that the Russells would be visiting Boston, and he requested, "The elder of the daughters I should wish you to

Invitation to attend the monthly meeting of the Bible Society, from Charles Cotesworth Pinckney to Nathaniel Russell, 1819.

The Russells were prominent among the city's civic leaders and philanthropists. They were also devout in their faith, and Mr. Russell served as treasurer of the Charleston Bible Society. He bequeathed $500 to the society in his will.

see a great deal of—she is much your inferior in years, But is inferior to few of [her] superiors in years in improvement."[9] Within a year of their move, Alicia married Arthur Middleton of Bolton Plantation on the Stono River. Middleton was the nephew and namesake of Arthur Middleton of Middleton Place, who was a signer of the Declaration of Independence.

The wedding of Alicia Russell and Arthur Middleton, which took place at the Russell House, was considered a highlight of the 1809 social season, for it united the crown princess of Charleston's merchant class with a son of one of the great planter families. The groom's aunt, Margaret Izard Manigault, wrote,

Arthur Middleton has been fortunate enough to select a very pleasing little woman for his mate. We must have thought so, had she possessed only her pretty countenance and soft winning manners. Her ample fortune ne nuit rien a la chose. There was a dance at the wedding. It was the first Ball the night after. There was a Ball at Mr. Gilchrist's. Mr. and Mrs. Henry Middleton gave a very pretty on Friday following. Mrs. Tom Middleton gives hers tomorrow. Mr. and Mrs. J. Manigault theirs on Friday. The Ball you see is kept up.[10]

After at least seven parties had been given to celebrate the marriage, Margaret Manigault's mother, Alice Delancey Izard, wrote back to her daughter that Arthur and Alicia must be tired of so much "show and splendor."[11]

The younger Russell daughter, Sarah, was also an accomplished lady who married well. In 1813, Sarah wed the Right Reverend Theodore Dehon, the rector of St. Michael's Church and second Episcopal bishop of South Carolina. This was a befitting match, as Sarah was known for her piety. Catherine Van Horne Read wrote to her sister in New York of the impending marriage:

[H]e is a very warm & ardent Lover. It is a union that promises as much happiness as any I ever heard of. Her whole life has been a series of piety. Faith & works in her have been united. Her immense fortune has enabled her to be very much the support of many poor families—thus you see his merits, his extraordinary goodness is like to be rewarded in this world as it most assuredly will be next.[12]

The couple greatly complemented each other's philanthropic interests. Bishop Dehon was an important leader in the early affairs of the church, and his untimely death was a source of great sadness to all who knew him. In 1817, only four years after his marriage to Sarah Russell, Dehon died of yellow fever. Sarah Russell Dehon returned to the Russell House with her three children to live with her mother.

PORTRAIT OF SARAH RUSSELL DEHON, **circa 1830, by Anne Izard McEuen (1809–1850). Pencil, charcoal, and watercolor on paper. Gift of Mrs. Henry Abbot, 92.5.5.**

Sarah Russell Dehon continued to live at the Russell House until her death in 1857. As a young widow, she championed many charitable causes.

In 1813, Sarah Russell married the Right Reverend Theodore Dehon, the rector of St. Michael's Church and the second Episcopal bishop of South Carolina. His untimely death—just four years after their marriage—was mourned throughout the city. In the Charleston Courier on August 7, 1817, one parishioner wrote, "The removal by death, of such a character, so much respected in his profession, esteemed by the public, and beloved in circles of private friendship and domestic life; is beyond the power of language to express!"

All three Russell ladies were known for their philanthropy. In 1813, Sarah Hopton Russell and her sister, Mary Christina Gregorie, helped found the Ladies Benevolent Society, which provided care to the sick and poor. Both Russell daughters were also active in the organization. The board of the Ladies Benevolent Society still meets annually in the Russell House. Working together in 1817, Sarah and her daughters established the Charleston Female Domestic Missionary Society, which ministered to the poor and slaves. The Domestic Missionary Society established St. Stephen's Chapel, which was one of the first churches in America built especially for the poor. St. Stephen's Chapel was constructed on land donated by Sarah Hopton Russell.

Nathaniel Russell died at the age of eighty-two. Paying homage to the loss of an esteemed member of the colonial generation, the *Charleston Courier* of April 12, 1820, eulogized Russell's departure:

> *DIED, yesterday, at his residence in Meeting-Street, the venerable NATHANIEL RUSSELL,—an upright, honorable man,—a philanthropist—and a fervent and exemplary christian. He was a native of New-England— an honor to the land which gave him birth—and a blessing to this city; which has long enjoyed the light of his virtues, the warmth of his benevolence, and the chastening purity of his character and influence.*[13]

Upon Sarah Russell's death in 1832, the house passed to their younger daughter, Sarah Russell Dehon. The house was filled with activity during the Dehon occupancy. Mrs. Dehon continued her mother's philanthropic and religious work. She shared the house with her son Theodore and his family, as well as her daughter Sarah and her husband, the Reverend Paul Trapier, and the Trapier's twelve children. In 1847, the Reverend Paul Trapier resigned the rectorship of St. Michael's Church and established Calvary Church as a place of worship for slaves. It was probably in the Russell House in 1855 that Trapier wrote the first Episcopal catechism published specifically for enslaved African Americans. The house was filled with Sarah Russell Dehon's children and grandchildren, who probably occupied the third-floor bedchambers. At that time a first-floor pantry and second-floor nursery were added to the back of the house.

Nathaniel Russell's family lived in his house for roughly fifty years—from 1808 until 1857. Following Sarah Russell Dehon's death, her children sold the property to Governor and Mrs. Robert Francis Withers Allston for $38,000. At that time, in a letter to Mrs. Allston, Henry Deas Lesesne described the house as "beyond all comparison, the finest establishment in Charleston."[14]

Enslaved African Americans and the Russell Family

According to the 1800 census, there were approximately eighteen slaves living with the Russells at their East Bay residence prior to their move to 51 Meeting Street. However, the 1810 and 1820 censuses do not shed any light on the number of enslaved Africans and African Americans living at the Russell House. From Russell family letters we know the names of at least some of the Russell slaves: David the houseboy, Diana, Hannah, "Mauma" the nurse, Phoebe, Rinchy Edwards, Simon, and Thomas Russell.

These enslaved workers were highly trained in the different skills required to run a property of the size and refinement of the Russell House. Domestic servants may have included a butler, several footmen, personal maids for members of the family, a nurse for the children, plus laundresses, seamstresses, cooks, and occasionally a pastry chef. The African American butler supervised the household under Mrs. Russell's direction. Slaves also maintained the grounds and stables as trained gardeners, hostlers, and carriage drivers. Slaves with specialized skills, such as carpenters, cabinetmakers, blacksmiths, and brick masons, were often hired out to work around the city for additional income for their owners. Sometimes the slaves received part of their earnings.

We know the Russells owned at least one slave who was hired out, Thomas Russell, who worked as a blacksmith along the wharves on East Bay Street. What little is known about Thomas Russell has been gleaned from his alleged involvement in the Denmark Vesey conspiracy. Russell was accused, convicted, and hanged for taking part in the supposed slave insurrection led by Vesey, a free black carpenter. In December 1823, Sarah Russell petitioned for the loss of her valued slave craftsman. Presumably, Thomas Russell generated much revenue for the Russells, providing blacksmithing services to shipping businesses along the waterfront. In testimony at the Vesey conspiracy trial, a Mrs. Marks placed Thomas Russell in proximity to Sarah Russell on a regular basis. She stated, "Mrs. Russel [sic] the prisoner's owner told me that Gullah Jack was constantly with Tom at breakfast, dinner, and supper, and that she cautioned Tom not to have so much to do with Jack or he would be taken up."[15] From this passage, we can infer that Thomas Russell lived at 51 Meeting Street and that the slaves took their meals in the kitchen dependency. This glimpse into the lives of the Russell slaves also hints at a certain level of freedom of movement and social interaction.

Dependencies from the south, 1979. Photograph courtesy of the Library of Congress, HABS SC, 10-CHAR, 2A-1.

While the Russells planted a formal garden in front of the property, the back lot contained a paved work yard that separated the main house from the service buildings. Of these structures, the two-story brick kitchen and laundry building remain and were linked via a hyphen to the main house in the nineteenth century. Now demolished, the large two-story brick carriage house, stable, and livestock sheds that housed cows and chickens were located to the rear of the yard. Enslaved Africans and African Americans lived in rooms directly above the kitchen and stable.

FLATWARE, **London, 1856–57, by George Adams of Chawner and Company. Silver, monogrammed: "RFWA" for Robert Francis Withers Allston. Historic Charleston Foundation purchase, 96.1.6–14.**

The Allston Occupation

In 1857, a year after Robert Francis Withers Allston was elected governor of the state of South Carolina, he and his family moved into the stately mansion at 51 Meeting Street. Governor Allston maintained vast landholdings throughout the Pee Dee region of South Carolina, primarily in the Georgetown district, and he had made his fortune as a rice planter. Governor Allston was quite an accomplished agriculturalist and wrote the well-regarded treatises *Memoir of the Introduction and Planting of Rice in South-Carolina* (1843) and *Essay on Sea Coast Crops* (1854). At the time of the Civil War, he owned more than 13,500 acres of land, and his slaveholdings totaled close to seven hundred individuals.[16]

Upon moving into the Russell House, the Allstons transformed the residence and garden into a high Victorian showplace, purchasing fashionable carpets, ceramics, fabrics, furniture, and silver. They probably selected the silver flatware by George William Adams of Chawner and Company of London in the Renaissance revival pattern for their new house. Stamped with the date letters for 1856–57, the silver is monogrammed "RFWA" for Robert Francis Withers Allston. At this time, the Allstons also updated the house's infrastructure by installing gas lighting, "hot water pipes," and interior water closets that replaced the outdoor privy.[17]

The Civil War began four years after the Allstons moved into their mansion, and the family was forced to evacuate Charleston. A trusted slave, Daddy Moses, was left behind to keep watch over the house and possessions that the family could not carry with them. Elizabeth Allston Pringle described their frantic departure to Society Hill, South Carolina:

> *It was a terrible undertaking to pack all that big, heavy furniture and get it away under stress. We found afterward that we had left many things of great value. At this moment I remember especially two blue Chinese vases, urn shaped, which stood two feet high and were very heavy. It seemed impossible to get boxes and material to pack them and they were left. Daddy Moses remained alone to take charge of the house and garden.[18]*

Soon after the family's departure, Daddy Moses died of a stroke while tending the garden. Prior to the Civil War, the Allston household included a number of slaves besides Daddy Moses. Again, from Elizabeth Allston Pringle's accounts, we know the names of some of these individuals, including Nelson Thompson, a house servant, and his wife Nelly, the laundress; William Barron, Daddy Moses's son who later became a caterer and cook; Stephen Gallant, Governor Allston's personal servant and valet; Joe Washington, the cook; maids Phoebe and Nanny; and an errand boy named Harris.[19]

During the war, life was greatly disrupted for all. Charleston was blockaded and placed under siege. Repeated bombardments threatened the entire southern end of the peninsula. The Russell House was in range of the Union cannon fire and three shells came through the roof, damaging the stair hall ceiling and much of the plaster on the third floor. Historian and archaeologist Martha Zierden wrote, "Although the damage caused by these shells was limited, the impact of the War on the city was nonetheless profound."[20] The city's cultural and built landscape was forever altered, and for families such as the Allstons this change resulted in great hardship.

While his family retreated to Society Hill during much of the Civil War, Governor Allston for the most part remained in Georgetown, South Carolina, where he caught pneumonia. On April 7, 1864, he died at Chicora Wood plantation, leaving his wife Adele and children to return to the Russell House alone after the fighting ceased.

After the Civil War, like so many Charleston families, the Allstons experienced great financial reversals. Adele Allston, as a result, opened a girls' school to help support her family. Her daughter Elizabeth Allston Pringle reported:

> *Preparations for the school are going on apace. We have moved into our house and it is too beautiful. I had forgotten how lovely it was. Fortunately, the beautiful paper in the second floor, the two drawing rooms and Mamma's room, has not been at all injured. The school is to open Jan. 1st and, strange to say Mamma is receiving letters from all over the State asking terms, etc. I thought there would be no applications, every one being so ruined by the War, but Mamma's name and personality make people anxious to give their daughters the benefit of her influence; and I suppose, the people in the cotton country are not so completely ruined and without money as we rice planters of the low country are. Be it as it may, the limit Mamma put of ten boarding pupils is nearly reached already.*[21]

By 1869, her school a success, Adele Allston decided to return to the country and allow her son Petigru Allston to plant rice. With her meager funds, she restored the family's Chicora Wood plantation near Georgetown. The Allstons then sold their Charleston mansion to the Sisters of Charity of Our Lady of Mercy for $19,000 in 1870.

Sisters of Charity of Our Lady of Mercy

The Sisters of Charity of Our Lady of Mercy, a Catholic order, had arrived in Charleston in 1829 and had been housed in various locations throughout the city. In 1870, they garnered funds from the

Front view of the Academy of Our Lady of Mercy, circa 1898. Courtesy of The Charleston Museum.

The Sisters of Charity of Our Lady of Mercy occupied the Russell House from 1870 to 1908. The house was noted for its beautifully maintained gardens with oleanders that "reach up to the curious iron balconies that are woven into the monogram of the builder," English box, crape myrtles, large orange and grapefruit trees, pomegranates, spikenard, tamarisk, and larkspur.

Frances Ravenel Smythe Edmunds receiving the Louise du Pont Crowninshield Award in 1971 from the National Trust for Historic Preservation.

A true visionary in the field of preservation, Frances Ravenel Smythe Edmunds was instrumental in the creation of Historic Charleston Foundation. In 1948, she became the first paid employee when she was hired as the director of the Festival of Houses Tour, a position that she transformed into the executive director of the Foundation. During her 37 years of service with the Foundation, she remained vigilant regarding the architectural legacy of Charleston and the Lowcountry by developing groundbreaking preservation initiatives. Already a leader in the Charleston community, her efforts were nationally recognized when she was appointed by President Carter to the Advisory Council on Historic Preservation.

federal government to purchase the house and large lot at 51 Meeting Street. Using the Russell House as their headquarters, they expanded the role of their school, the Academy of Our Lady of Mercy. The number of students attending the school ranged from 85 to 120, and 8 teachers lived in the house.

During the Sisters' occupancy, the building received damage during the earthquake of 1886—it was described as "badly sprung" while the outbuildings were "badly cracked."[22] After the earthquake, all of the structures on the property were anchored and bolted and the outbuildings underwent a series of changes.

In 1901, the academy moved to Calhoun Street and the mansion served as the order's mother house until 1908. Shortly thereafter, the sisters sold the property to Dr. Lane and Mrs. Caroline Hampton Lowndes Mullally. After almost forty years, the Nathaniel Russell House once again became a private residence. The Mullallys made extensive changes to the house and maintained the beautiful gardens. In 1913, Mr. Francis J. and Mrs. Mary Roscoe Randolph Pelzer purchased the property and they further altered the building to suit modern conveniences.

From Private Residence to Foundation Headquarters and House Museum

When Historic Charleston Foundation (HCF) purchased the property from the Pelzer family in 1955, the acquisition constituted a dramatic change in course for the nascent preservation organization, which just a few years prior had proclaimed that "the Foundation was not concerned with House Museums."[23]

Threatened by site development, HCF rallied local and national support during a ten-day blitz campaign to rescue the property. Stories of schoolchildren donating bags of pennies earned from the sale of lemonade demonstrated the community's passion for both the house and the Foundation's preservation mission. The small staff at HCF was obviously not alone in recognizing that 51 Meeting Street was one of the most architecturally and historically significant houses in Charleston.

Although a house museum strayed from the Foundation's original mission, opening the Nathaniel Russell House to the public proved to be a fortuitous decision. The house also served as the Foundation's first permanent office and headquarters, becoming so entwined with HCF's identity that images of the Russell House were synonymous with the institution's preservation efforts. In the words of historian Robert R. Weyeneth, "For four decades the property housed and funded the foundation, giving it the resources to pursue a far-flung preservation agenda in Charleston and the surrounding Lowcountry."[24] This initiative established HCF as a commanding presence in the preservation world, and early efforts to decorate an antebellum town house morphed into a nationally renowned museum collection.

ARMCHAIR (ONE IN A SET), **England, circa 1800. Wood painted black with gilt decoration. Gift of Benjamin Allston Moore Jr. and Mr. and Mrs. B.H. Rutledge Moore in honor of their parents, Benjamin Allston and Susan Middleton Rutledge Moore, 92.2.2.** *Photograph by Russell Buskirk.*

This English fancy chair descended in the family of Governor Robert F.W. Allston, who purchased 51 Meeting Street from the Russell family in 1857.

Initially, one of HCF's greatest challenges was furnishing an empty house in preparation for public viewing. The Furnishings and Decoration Committee, chaired by Josephine Pinckney from 1958 to 1973, was appointed to tackle the daunting task of assembling a museum collection—without any purchase funds. Once again the community rallied in support of HCF, and friends of the Foundation loaned or gifted fine and decorative arts to adorn the interior of the Russell House. These early efforts were the beginnings of today's museum collection.

The Russell House now serves as an ideal exhibition space for HCF's outstanding collection of fine and decorative arts. While wealthy planters and merchants such as Nathaniel Russell were known for importing great quantities of goods from abroad, they also decorated their residences with fine furnishings made in Charleston. Over the past fifty-three years, the Foundation has acquired key holdings, the majority with local provenances.

Historic Charleston Foundation Festival of Houses and Gardens Poster, 1958.

From 1955 until 1992, the Russell House served as Historic Charleston Foundation's headquarters, functioning as the center of operations for the Foundation's preservation initiatives for thirty-seven years.

Among the eighteenth- and nineteenth-century artifacts are paintings and works on paper by some of America's and Europe's most well-known artists, such as Henry Benbridge; fine furniture crafted in Charleston, including German cabinetmaker Jacob Sass's monumental desk and bookcase; and rare silver and porcelain.

Through the years, the HCF collection continued to grow, and the Russell House garnered national recognition for its historical significance, receiving the National Historic Landmark designation in 1974. However, by the early 1990s, it was quite obvious that the building, which had served the Foundation so well for forty years, was now in need of great attention. In 1992, management of the Russell House dramatically shifted, and a new era of inquiry and study was initiated. The Foundation moved its headquarters and, for the first time, the site was operated entirely as a house museum. Within the next five years, HCF embarked upon a major restoration project following a detailed architectural, archaeological, and documentary analysis of the site. A team of nationally renowned experts, along with HCF staff, and funding from the Getty Foundation helped return the Russell House to its 1808 grandeur. Today, the house and grounds are symbolic of HCF's commitment to preserving Charleston's built environment and material culture.

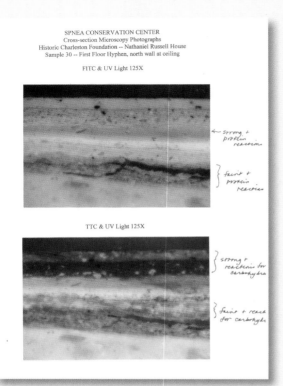

Example of microscopic paint analysis from Susan L. Buck's VOLUME V: CROSS-SECTION MICROSCOPY PAINT STUDY, NATHANIEL RUSSELL HOUSE, AN ARCHITECTURAL AND HISTORICAL ANALYSIS OF THE NATHANIEL RUSSELL HOUSE**, Charleston, SC, December 1996.**

In 1995, the Foundation was awarded a J.P. Getty Foundation Architectural Conservation Grant to research the interiors of the Nathaniel Russell House with the goal of returning the house to its 1808 appearance. Cross sections of paint samples are studied in different lights under a microscope to determine the original color and age of the decorative finishes. These findings were compiled to create a report that would guide restoration of the house.

Interior, pre-restoration.

The draperies and furniture seen in this photograph were the result of the Furnishings and Decoration Committee's decisions established in the late 1950s. Groundbreaking research and careful analysis of Federal-style room inventories concluded that the space was originally used as a dining room.

Drawing room cornice during conservation and restoration treatment, late 1990s.

Using information obtained through microscopic paint analysis, the elaborate composition and cast-plaster cornices of the drawing room were restored to their 1808 grandeur, showing the richness of color and texture chosen by Russell throughout.

Original trompe l'oeil painted cornice, third-floor bedroom.

When conservators removed portions of the twentieth-century ornamental plaster, they uncovered a neoclassical trompe l'oeil cornice. Research suggested that Samuel O'Hara, who moved to Charleston from Baltimore, was responsible for painting several of the early decorative surfaces in the house. As advertised in the *Charleston Courier* on May 14, 1808, O'Hara encouraged prospective clients to visit "Mr. Russell's new building in Meeting Street, for specimen of his work, which he confidently believes has not been equaled by any in the city."

Entry room.

Mercantile correspondents or tradesmen engaged in business with Russell would have been received in the entry room by an enslaved butler. The floor cloth is a reproduction by Period Designs (Yorktown, Virginia). The leaf motif, most likely tobacco, was derived from an 1807 plat drawing by John Diamond of Charleston, who advertised that he made floor cloths as well as surveyed land.

Entrance Hall and Office

During Nathaniel Russell's time, guests entered the house via an entry room or waiting area. One of the slaves, serving as a butler, would have greeted visitors at the front door and welcomed them into the house. If arriving to see Nathaniel Russell on business and not a close associate, family member, or friend, the visitor would have waited in the entry hall and then perhaps would have entered into the small room to the south, which served as an office.

Subsequent occupants often found uses for spaces in the house that were different from Mr. and Mrs. Russell's. Rooms were adapted to meet the needs of the current residents. Sarah Russell Dehon, according to her 1857 probate inventory, converted the front office into a bedroom. In the twentieth century, the wall separating the entry and office was removed to create one large foyer. Research and architectural evidence uncovered in 1994 confirmed that the entry was originally divided into two spaces, and HCF replaced the south wall.

Period inventories suggest that entry rooms would have been plainly furnished with items similar to those exhibited today, including the reproduction painted floor cloth, a barometer, and a set of Windsor chairs. The chairs are reproductions modeled after the bow-back Windsor chair with faux bamboo turnings that is currently exhibited in Nathaniel Russell's office. Stamped on the underside by the Philadelphia craftsman Thomas Mason, the side chair descended in the Nathaniel Russell family and is possibly an original Russell House furnishing. Mason shipped Windsor chairs to Charleston from 1803 to 1809. Paint analysis indicates that the chair was originally painted brick red with white turnings, and the reproductions in the entry room replicate the original.

Other furnishings in the entry room and office relate to Russell's endeavors as a merchant or the public nature of the space. The simple turned and joined stretcher table, made for Daniel Huger's Limerick Plantation, is one of the few extant examples of Lowcountry furniture from the early eighteenth century. The desk and bookcase is also a rarity, as it is the only documented case furnishing signed by Jacob Sass. Sass inscribed an interior drawer: "Made by Jacob Sass—Charleston/ Octr. 1794—£25—JS." The well-crafted desk and bookcase may have been made for Mary Motte and her husband William Allston, who lived in the Miles Brewton House on King Street. William Allston was an ancestor of Governor R.F.W. Allston, who purchased 51 Meeting Street from the Russell family.[25]

Some spectacular maps are also displayed in the entry room and office, including Herman Moll's *A New and Exact Map of the Dominions of the King of Great Britain*, dated 1715. Moll's map, which

Office.

Russell would have carried out tasks related to his mercantile endeavors from his office. The simple cypress stretcher table (circa 1715) has a Limerick Plantation provenance and is characteristic of early furniture made in the French Santee area, just outside of Charleston. The monumental desk and bookcase was made in the workshop of Charleston cabinetmaker Jacob Sass (German born, 1750–1836) in 1794, as evidenced by his signature in a drawer. Crafted by Thomas Mason of Philadelphia, the bow-back Windsor chair is believed to have been an original Russell House furnishing.

descended in the Kennedy family of Charleston, includes a depiction of early Charleston's walled city. Much later in date, Edmund Petrie's 1788 survey of Charleston was engraved and published as the *Ichnography of Charleston, South-Carolina: at the request of Adam Tunno, Esq., for the use of the Phoenix Fire-Company of London.* This rare print was one of the first fire insurance company maps of an American city to be published. A third map, *South Carolina including Charleston*, was engraved circa 1802 by the well-known local artist Thomas Coram (working circa 1770–1811).

The glazed double doors with fanlight above are the most notable architectural feature in the entry room. Delicate composition beading was used to enrich the muntins and transom. The composition ornament, while decorative, also gave strength and flexibility to the glazed portion of the door, allowing for the use of complex geometric shapes. The doors were originally faux grained and have been returned to their former magnificence. Even if a visitor was not ushered past the entry room's doors into the family's domain, one could look through the glass panels to see the splendor within the Russell mansion.

Stair Hall

The free-flying staircase continues to impress guests of the Nathaniel Russell House two hundred years after it was built. Despite centuries of hurricanes, earthquakes, and wars, the cantilevered stairs survive as a testament to Charleston's rich architectural heritage—and the restoration of the stair hall itself became a symbol of preservation advocacy in the city.

During HCF's research phase to return the Russell House to its 1808 appearance, the team revealed traces of a trompe l'oeil cornice in the stair hall. The conservators also discovered that the original paint scheme incorporated a different cornice design on each floor. Following preservation standards, artisans painted reproductions of each cornice on canvas, which were then applied to the wall rather than destroying the nineteenth-century material below.

Paint analysis throughout the Russell House revealed that the residence originally featured a wide variety of faux decorative finishes. Elaborate color schemes and faux finishes imitating stone and wood were popular decorative luxuries during the Federal period. All the interior pine doors in the house were painted to resemble imported fine woods and would have made a dramatic statement of the family's taste and wealth to their guests. Documentary evidence suggests that these painted decorations were the work of local artisan Samuel O'Hara.

An Ornate Entry.

Social hierarchy was of great importance in Charleston society, and only friends and invited guests would have been escorted from the entry room through the elaborately glazed doors to the stair hall. The doors contain the original glass; however, several panes are deteriorating, a process known as crizzling.

Detail of stairs.

The flying staircase ascends from the first to the third floor without any visible means of support.

Above: MARY RUTLEDGE SMITH WITH SON EDWARD NUTT SMITH, **London, circa 1786, by George Romney (1734–1802). Oil on canvas. Historic Charleston Foundation purchase, 77.1.1.**

In 1786, while visiting England with her husband Colonel Roger Smith on their grand tour, Mary Rutledge Smith (b. 1747) sat for the famous English portraitist George Romney. She is seen here holding her son Edward. The painting was exhibited throughout the nineteenth century, and it was publicly viewed at the Carolina Art Association in 1884 for the last time before it was sold at auction in England five years later. In the late 1970s, the painting was again sent to auction and purchased on behalf of HCF.

Left: **Stair hall.**

The free-flying staircase is the most impressive architectural feature in the Russell House. Built on the cantilever principle, each step is supported by those below and by each landing. The sinuous curve of the handrails is formed by hundreds of mitered and joined sections of Honduran mahogany.

The mahogany tall clock in the stair hall descended in the Nathaniel Russell Paine family of Charleston, who were distant relatives and close friends of Nathaniel Russell. The works and case of the clock were made in England in 1770 and the face bears the name "Joshua Lockwood, Charles Town." Lockwood arrived in Charleston from London and referred to himself as a clockmaker, but there is no evidence that he made any of the clock's elements or cases. It is speculated that Lockwood's clock faces arrived from London already engraved.

Dining Room

During the Russell and Allston family occupations, the elliptical room on the first floor served as a dining room. Later in the history of the house, the room became a library and was initially interpreted as such by HCF until research revealed its earlier function. The concept of a space specifically devoted to the act of dining was relatively new when the house was built and was only codified during Russell's lifetime. The desire for comfort and luxury resulted in the increased specialization of both objects and living spaces. Designers such as Robert Adam helped make the dining room a standard feature in the neoclassical house and the dinner party became a major form of entertainment.

Charlestonians were known for their hospitality and love of luxury, and the Russells and Allstons would have hosted many grand dinner parties in the dining room. Typically after these social gatherings, women would have retired to a separate room, such as the lavish drawing room upstairs, while the men remained in the dining room and enjoyed wine, spirits, and punch. In Charleston, the main meal of the day usually took place at approximately two or three o'clock in the afternoon, and, depending on the occasion, may have lasted for upward of three hours. Charlestonians preferred dining *à l'anglais*—where all food in the course was placed on the table at once—long after service *à la française* became popular elsewhere. Service *à la française*, in which the meal was served plate by plate, required much more of a slave presence in the dining room because more people were needed to facilitate a lavish dinner in that manner. As the dining room was a place where political affairs were often discussed, the increasing fear in Charleston of slave insurrection may have influenced the popularity of dining *à l'anglais*.[26]

The dining table is currently set in the *à l'anglais* manner. Guests, facilitated by the help of a butler, would have been served and then helped themselves from the covered dishes, tureens, and platters symmetrically placed on the dining table. Covered silver vegetable dishes made by New York silversmith Peter Chitry (working circa 1812–circa 1836), flatware by various English

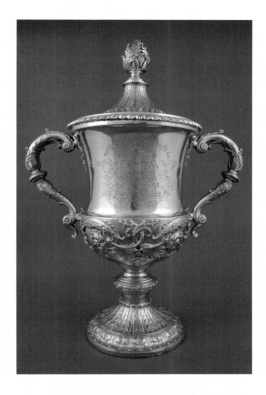

TWO-HANDLED CUP WITH COVER, **London, 1769, by John Swift (apprenticeship completed, 1725). Silver with later gilt. Gift of Mr. James P. Barrow, 97.5.1.** *Photograph by Russell Buskirk.*

This two-handled cup is based upon an example commissioned in 1736 by Colonel James Pelham from the architect and designer William Kent. The arms are those of Governor William Bull II (1710–91) of Charleston, a close associate and friend of Nathaniel Russell. The engraved armorial design incorporates the Bull family motto, *Ducit amor patriae* (love of country leads).

Above: CARD TABLE, **Charleston, circa 1800. Mahogany with satinwood inlay and églomisé decoration. Historic Charleston Foundation collection fund purchase, 2001.001.005.**

Right: **Card table detail.**
Detail of the Charleston-made card table showing the inset églomisé, or reverse painted glass.

makers, and a rare cruet stand by Hester Bateman (1708–1794) with its original silver capped bottles adorn the table. Much of the silver descended in the Allston, Frost, Gregorie, and Middleton families of Charleston. The handsome silver spoons, engraved *JMCG*, belonged to Sarah Hopton Russell's brother-in-law and sister, James and Mary Christiana Hopton Gregorie. In 1823, Mary Gregorie bequeathed her silver to her niece, Alicia Hopton Russell Middleton, and many of these items are now exhibited at the Russell House.

The dining table, sideboard, card table with églomisé insets, and Pembroke table were all made in Charleston in the late eighteenth century. While the chairs appear to be from the same set, half were made in New York and the remainder were made locally, attesting to the prevalence and use of pattern books. The sideboard, although used for storing bottles of wine and Madeira as well as items for the dinner service, was primarily a place to show off one's finest silver.

Detailed analysis revealed that the wall plaster in the dining room was original and that the surface was never painted, suggesting that it was always meant to be papered. In the late 1990s, a small fragment of the original verditer blue wallpaper was found behind a bell pull, and the paper was reproduced to decorate the room. An appropriate period wallpaper border with an interlocking ring design has also been added. Many of the original elements from the Russell occupation are present, including the door and window hardware and mantel with carved pilasters, applied composition ornament, and center frieze depicting a Bacchic scene.

Dining room.

At present, the Charleston-made dining table is set for six, but in the event of a larger dinner party the mahogany table could expand to accommodate 18 guests. Flatware once belonging to James and Mary Christiana Gregorie, Sarah Hopton Russell's sister and brother-in-law, adorns the table, along with Chinese export dinnerware in the "Peacock and Peony" pattern popular in late eighteenth-century Charleston.

Detail of the breakfast table.

Although many American ships ventured to Asia after the Revolutionary War, Nathaniel Russell's ship, the *Russell*, owned in partnership with the Newport, Rhode Island firm of Gibbs and Channing, is the only documented eighteenth-century vessel known to have engaged in the China trade directly from Charleston. The *Russell* sailed from the city in the spring of 1796 and returned the following year with a hold full of blue-and-white export porcelain, lacquered wares, tea, and silk. The ship's captain, William Wood, sought the services of Canton's leading porcelain merchant, Syngchong, from whom he purchased more than ten thousand pieces of "Nankeen blue." During archaeological digs on the property, several shards of similar blue-and-white china were unearthed.

Back Parlor

When the Mullallys purchased the house in 1909, the family enlarged the back parlor to create a formal dining room. During HCF's restoration of the house, experts chose to install a partition wall to return the room to its original square proportions. Research shows that the walls were whitewashed in 1808, while the furniture and carpet were probably blue in color, as this room is referred to in family diaries as the "Blue Room." The table is set with blue and white Chinese export porcelain, which would have been used by the family for breakfast and other informal meals. In 1796, Nathaniel Russell imported a great deal of blue-and-white porcelain along with other goods into Charleston aboard his ship, the *Russell*, which is the only known eighteenth-century vessel to sail from Charleston directly to China. The goods that Russell imported were advertised for purchase in the local paper.

The back parlor would not only have been used for casual dining, but also served as a family room. From the back parlor, Mrs. Russell may have overseen household operations and managed her personal daily activities. As founders of the Ladies Benevolent Society in 1813, Mrs. Russell and her two daughters hosted several of the organization's meetings in their house. HCF is fortunate to have the mahogany charity box from the Ladies Benevolent Society exhibited in the back parlor. Today the Ladies Benevolent Society continues to serve those in need.

Drawing Room

Following the tradition of the *piano nobile* used in English Palladian architecture, the second floor of the Russell House features the most socially important rooms. The oval drawing room was wallpapered with an expensive paper, probably imported from France or England. Conservators chose the wall color based on a small sample that was discovered underneath the floorboards. Paint analysis concluded that

Back parlor.

As the informal living space, the back parlor contrasts with the formal drawing rooms on the second floor. Both the Charleston desk and bookcase and the box to its left are on loan from two of the city's most venerable societies. The South Carolina Society's desk and bookcase has the characteristic figure-eight fretwork so popular in eighteenth- and early nineteenth-century Charleston. Similar figure-eight decoration can be seen on the architraves in the withdrawing room. The box is on loan from the Ladies Benevolent Society.

the cornice in the room was dramatically painted with ox blood red and grisaille, a style of painting using gray tints to create a dramatic effect of dimensions. The beading and drops were gilded in twenty-two-karat gold leaf and a yellow wash. The doors have been regrained to mahogany, with ebony and satinwood inlay on the landing side and burled wood or tortoiseshell on those sides facing inward. In each room, a paint history has been preserved for future study.

Elizabeth Allston Pringle reminisced about the drawing room in *Chronicles of Chicora Wood*:

> *There were four large windows on the south, opening on the iron balcony, which ran round on the outside. And, on the opposite side of the room, two windows exactly like those opening on the balcony, running from the tall ceiling to the floor, but the panes of these were mirrors. It made you think you were looking into another crowded room.*[27]

The mirrored panels were designed to reflect light and give the impression of a larger room. Lighting in the early nineteenth century was expensive and used sparingly. Polished gilt surfaces on furniture and architectural moldings, as well as mirrors, reflected light throughout the impressive room.

The sumptuous surroundings of the drawing room were the perfect setting for post-dinner entertainment. Ladies in the nineteenth century were expected to be proficient at playing musical instruments such as the pianoforte, the harp, or the lyre guitar. Today the room features a mahogany pianoforte made by Longman and Broderip of London, dating to 1790. The piano stool with gilt painting was probably made in England as well, but is of later construction than the piano. The lyre guitar, also English, is from the late eighteenth century.

During the neoclassical period, Greco-Roman motifs—themes often associated with art and music—could be found throughout the houses of the elite, particularly in the drawing rooms. The French engraving *Apollo et Les Muses* by Jules Romain, dating to 1816, hangs

Detail of cornice.
The frieze of this elaborately enriched cornice is loosely taken from Batty and Thomas Langley's *Gothic Architecture*, published in London in 1742 and 1747. In 1955, original pendants, mistaken for Victorian additions, were removed from the cornice yet fortunately survived in storage until they were restored during the 1990s.

Drawing room.

In June 1863, just before the family evacuated the city, Adele Allston, daughter of Governor R.F.W. Allston and his wife, married Arnoldus Vanderhorst. The ceremony took place in the Russell House drawing room. Adele Allston's sister, Elizabeth, described the occasion in *Chronicles of Chicora Wood*. Providing a vivid description of "our oval drawing-room or ballroom," she wrote that the room "was papered in white with small sprigs of golden flowers scattered over it. There were four large windows on the south, opening on the iron balcony which ran around on the outside. And, on the opposite side of the room, two windows exactly like those opening on the balcony…but the panes of these were mirrors. It made you think you were looking into another crowded room."

above the drawing room mantel. While listening to the classical music, guests would have been seated in furniture such as the Grecian-inspired recamier and lyre-back chairs exhibited in the room.

Withdrawing Room

As the second grandest room in the Russell House, the architectural detailing in the withdrawing room is rivaled only by that in the adjacent drawing room. The two rooms are now joined by a shared door; however, in Russell's time a closet for china and other serving accoutrements was located in place of the small passage. The withdrawing room door, window surrounds, and the mantel decoration are all composition ornament. Before undergoing conservation, the details of the elaborate ornamental cornice had been obscured with more than sixteen layers of paint. Traces of twenty-two-karat gold gilt were uncovered through the microscopic paint analysis process, and now the grandeur of the cornice has been restored. The cast-plaster cornice frieze merits comparison with the work of Placido Columbani, whose 1776 book *A Variety of Capitals, Friezes and Cornickes…* was identified in the estate of one of Charleston's stucco workers.

In the Russells' and Allstons' time, the withdrawing room was a place to gather friends and family for both formal and informal entertainments. Decorative arts related to taking tea, letter writing, and card playing—common leisure activities—are now exhibited in the room,

Above: **Detail of mirrored windows.**
The mirrored panels in elaborate surrounds of carved wood with applied composition ornament reflect sunlight and candlelight, which further highlight the dramatic color scheme in the room.

Left: **Detail of drawing room faux bois.**
After numerous layers of paint were removed from the interior of the drawing room doors, the original burl wood faux graining was revealed.

Withdrawing room.

Several notable examples of Charleston fine and decorative arts are exhibited in the withdrawing room. Samuel F.B. Morse painted the portrait of Charlestonian Susannah Branford Hayne Smilie, circa 1820, while the artist was on one of his many visits to the city. Nathaniel Russell Middleton, grandson of Nathaniel Russell, exhibited his painting *Group of Cherubs* at the Carolina Art Association exhibition in 1858. His daughter, Alicia Hopton Middleton, later donated the painting to the Gibbes Museum of Art, and it is now on loan to the Foundation.

Detail of the molding and cornices.

Cast plaster and composition ornament, such as foliage-enriched moldings, garlands, palmettes, urns, and scrolled base moldings are employed throughout the Russell House and were derived, but not precisely copied, from the published works of architects and designers Robert Adam, Placido Columbani, and William Pain. Pattern books were widely available during the Federal period.

including several notable examples of Charleston-made furniture in the early neoclassical style. The settee is one of only six documented from the period. Among the other outstanding locally crafted furnishings in the withdrawing room are a pair of elliptical-front card tables with bold geometric inlays, a Pembroke table with delicate string inlay and oval paterae adorned with sprouting foliage, and an urn stand. The Pembroke table is set as if the ladies were sitting down to tea. Of the various accoutrements associated with tea drinking in America, the urn stand is the rarest of extant items, and is one of only two documented Charleston-made examples. Although a seemingly modest object, the urn stand represented the epitome of fashion and sophistication in the eighteenth century. Silver hot water urns, costly items found in only the wealthiest American households, were placed upon the stands adjacent to the tea table. The hot water urn that HCF displays on the stand is engraved with the coat of arms of the Kinloch family. Both the stand and the urn were functional but specialized, superfluous forms, and therefore their use was a display of their owner's wealth and refinement.

Bedchamber

One of four bedrooms in the Russell House, the second-floor bedchamber is the most elaborate and was likely used by the master and mistress of the house. Guests of both the Russells and Allstons would have been welcomed into the room during intimate gatherings of close friends as well as large parties. Thus, it was important that the best bedchamber was richly decorated and furnished, especially in comparison to the secondary bedrooms on the third floor.

Today, one exits the second-floor bedroom and can proceed down a back staircase that was built in the twentieth century to replace the narrow, winding servants' stair that spiraled from the first floor to the attic. The original staircase provided access for the domestic help to quietly move through the different parts of the house. It still exists from the third floor to the attic. Originally, a square dressing room accessed through a door on the left side of the fireplace occupied the area adjacent to the bedchamber. The dressing room would also have been the most appropriate place to keep an easy chair such as the one exhibited in the bedchamber. Made in Philadelphia, this type of chair, usually associated with the aged or infirm, also doubled as a "necessary" chair, as it has a chamber pot attached to the bottom. The privies were located at the farthest corners of the property and an easy chair would have been a great convenience to its owner. Enslaved house servants had the unpleasant chore of emptying the contents of the chamber pot each morning.

The current appearance of the second-floor bedchamber is the result of a restoration following Hurricane Hugo in 1989. The paint colors were based on analysis conducted in 1988; however, it is now believed that the light shades may be the second or third generation of paint. Like the rest of the house, the doors were grained to resemble mahogany. The wall-to-wall carpet is a reproduction Brussels carpet in a vermiculated design. The chintz bed and window hangings are also reproductions and were woven after a sample of early nineteenth-century English fabric. Called "Lord Byron Chintz," the whimsical and exotic pattern was adapted from the fabric that Lord Byron used for his own bed at Newstead Abbey, Nottinghamshire, England. The textiles adorn a handsome Charleston bedstead with an elaborate inlaid mahogany cornice. In the hot summer months, gauze mosquito netting would have replaced the bed curtains.

In addition to the bedstead, the handsome dressing chest and neoclassical secretary wardrobe were also made by highly skilled Charleston cabinetmakers. The exquisite secretary wardrobe, which descended in the family of John Rutledge, chief justice of the Federal Supreme Court during George Washington's administration, shows evidence of both British and New York design inspiration. The interior secretary drawer is fully faced with satinwood and retains its original ivory knobs.

Bedroom.

One of the four bedrooms in the house, this room was the best bedchamber, and common to many contemporary house plans, was located adjacent to the main entertaining spaces. Best bedchambers were decorated with rich textiles, as seen here. An adjoining dressing room was removed in the twentieth century and a modern stairwell was built to replace the small, winding servants' stairs.

Detail of double chest.

The figure-eight decoration was popular in Charleston and can also be seen on the mid-eighteenth-century desk and bookcase in the back parlor, as well as the moldings in the drawing room window surrounds.

DOUBLE CHEST, **Charleston, circa 1770. Mahogany with mahogany veneer, cypress, and mahogany secondary woods. Historic Charleston Foundation collection fund purchase, 2003.001.003.**

Both imported to and produced in Charleston, the chest-on-chest, or "double chest," was ubiquitous throughout the Lowcountry in the eighteenth century. Today it has come to characterize the high construction standards and quality of workmanship for which Charleston's colonial furniture is known. This outstanding example is one of only two documented Charleston double chests with quarter columns in the base and applied fretwork on the upper chamfers.

DRESSING CHEST, **Charleston, 1760s. Mahogany. Gift of Patricia Kinloch McCown, 81.7.1.** *Photograph by Russell Buskirk.*

In mid-eighteenth-century Charleston, dressing chests were the height of fashion. This example retains its original hardware and drawer fittings, including a hinged mirror and compartments with delicate wooden lids that would have contained the toiletries. Although dressing chests were commonly found in houses of the period, relatively few of these Charleston-made furnishings survive. This is a particularly outstanding example of the form.

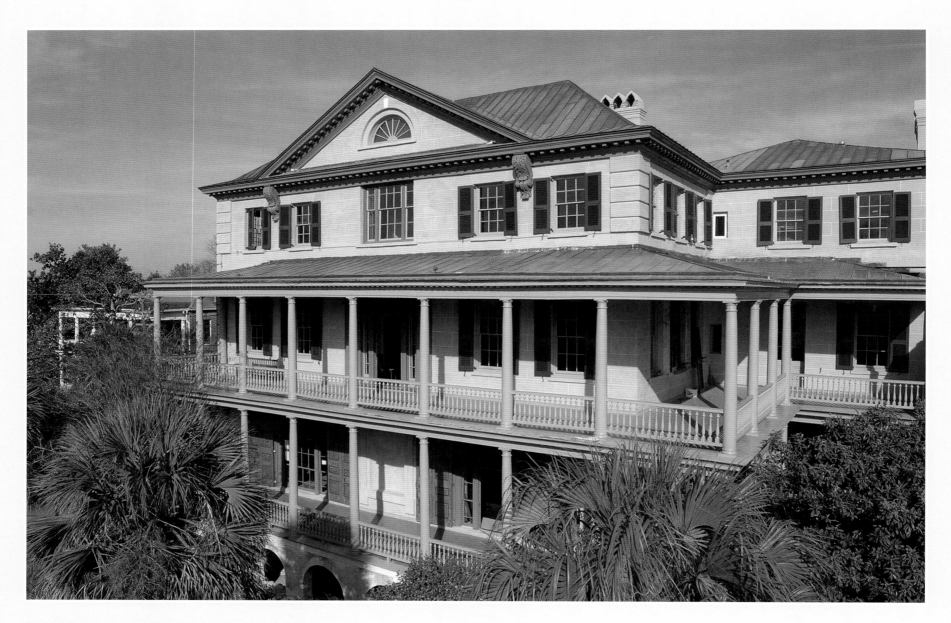

Aiken-Rhett House, 48 Elizabeth Street, Charleston, SC.

View of the exterior of the house from Judith Street. *Photograph by Carroll Ann Bowers.*

THE AIKEN-RHETT HOUSE, CIRCA 1820

48 Elizabeth Street

The Aiken-Rhett House is the most intact urban, antebellum town house complex in Charleston. Visitors to the property view preserved interiors that have survived virtually unaltered since the nineteenth century. The story of the Aiken-Rhett House and the people who lived there spans four generations and encompasses the most turbulent period in American history—the Civil War.

The Brief Tenure of John and Susan Robinson, 1820–1825

Built in 1820, the Aiken-Rhett House was the home of Charleston merchant John Robinson and his wife Susan. Originally constructed as a typical Charleston double house, the building had a central hallway with two rooms on either side. The main entrance was located on the south façade and guests ascended the stairs to the porch, known in Charleston as a piazza, and entered into the hallway. An 1825 newspaper advertisement described the house as containing "twelve upright rooms, four on each floor, all well finished, the materials of the piazzas and fences all of cypress and cedar; underneath the house are large cellars and storerooms."[28] The exterior appearance of the house was refined, but in a restrained fashion that included carefully matched Flemish bond brickwork and precise, white lime mortar joints, elegant proportions, and a two-story piazza above a brick arcade. The brickwork was given a rather monochromatic appearance by a thin coating of red wash. Also part of the property were two support buildings to the rear of the main house that contained a kitchen, slave quarters, stables, and possibly a carriage house.

John Robinson had made his fortune from mercantile endeavors, and he also invested in real estate. As early as 1817, he purchased property in Wraggborough, the neighborhood surrounding the Aiken-Rhett House. Robinson owned the lot on the corner of Elizabeth and Judith Streets by 1820, and it is believed that he began construction on the house that year. After only five years, however, Robinson was forced to sell the property to meet financial obligations when he lost the cargo of at least two ships at sea.

PORTRAIT OF JOHN F. ROBINSON **(1776–1849), artist and date unknown.**

The builder of the Aiken-Rhett House, Robinson was a successful merchant, land speculator, and factor. Along with business associate William Aiken Sr., he was a founding member of the Second Presbyterian Church on Meeting Street. *Courtesy of the estate of Elizabeth Robinson Geffckin.*

PORTRAIT OF SUSAN THOMAS ROBINSON
(1784–1858), artist and date unknown.

Susan Robinson, along with husband John
Robinson, is buried in the graveyard of the
Second Presbyterian Church of Charleston.
Courtesy of the estate of Elizabeth Robinson Geffckin.

Just eight days after Robinson's advertisement to sell his house appeared in the *Charleston Courier*, he mortgaged an extensive list of properties to Charles Edmondston, William S. Aiken Sr., and Lewis A. Pitray to secure a debt for the sum of $195,200. Hardly strangers, Robinson and Aiken were both active in civic affairs, serving on several committees together; and both were members of the board of directors of the South Carolina Canal and Rail Road Company. Aiken and Pitray took possession of the mortgaged property in October of 1826. In two transactions executed eight months later, William Aiken Sr. took sole possession of the house on the corner of Judith and Elizabeth Streets. Thus, the era of Aiken family ownership began and lasted over 150 years. By the time of his death in 1849, John Robinson had recovered financially, leaving plantations to his sons and property to his daughters and wife. Susan Robinson lived at 10 Judith Street, a residence adjacent to the Aiken-Rhett House, until her death in 1858.

The Aiken Family, 1827–1857

For William Aiken Sr., the acquisition of Robinson's grand house at 48 Elizabeth Street was an investment and not an opportunity for a change of residence. On July 12, 1827, just five weeks after assuming title of the Robinson properties, Aiken offered the house for sale, describing the property in terms similar to Robinson's 1825 newspaper advertisement.[29] The house did not sell and William Aiken Sr. used it as a rental property for the next four years. He made no known changes to the house or grounds during that time.

Aiken, who was an Irish immigrant, accumulated a large fortune and became one of the city's leading cotton merchants. He was also closely involved with the development of the South Carolina Canal and Rail Road Company, of which he was the first president. He kept that post from 1828 until his death in 1831, and under his direction, a route between Charleston and Hamburg, a boomtown near Augusta, was established. Unfortunately, he did not live to see the completion of these tracks. Aiken died in a carriage accident and his vast property was divided between his widow, Henrietta Wyatt Aiken (1785–1848), and their only child, William Aiken Jr. (1806–1887). Aiken Jr., who was twenty-five years old at the time of his father's death, had married Harriet Lowndes (1812–1892) just a month before.

In March 1833, William Aiken Jr. and his mother executed a deed in which the Robinson house was transferred to him. Now twenty-seven years old and in sole possession of the large brick house on a prominent site in Wraggborough, Aiken Jr. and his wife began transforming it into a grand Greek Revival–style mansion. Creating larger public rooms more suitable for entertaining, three main changes to the property took place in the early 1830s: the Aikens moved the front entrance to the west façade, reconfigured the first floor, and added a large addition to eastern portion of the house.

The Aikens abandoned the symmetry that had governed Robinson's Federal-style floor plan and embraced a more fluid layout that encouraged guests to wander through the public spaces on the first floor. Removing the front door from the Judith Street side of the house and building a rather large addition on the Elizabeth Street façade made a significant architectural statement. With the addition of the two-story wing to the east side, the entire house and the dependencies were covered with a coat of stucco. The stucco was scored in imitation of masonry blocks and coated with a yellow ochre finish set off by hand-painted white lines, which simulated mortar joints.

In 1835, the Aikens moved into their newly renovated house refashioned in the popular Greek Revival style.[30] The house was intended to make an impression, and the Aikens' success in that enterprise is reflected in a letter written by an unknown author to Francis Kinloch Middleton in February 1839:

MINIATURE OF WILLIAM AIKEN, **1829, by Savinien Edme Dubourjal (French). Watercolor on ivory. Gift of the heirs of Mary Green Maybank, 2000.3.20.**

A typical grand tour souvenir for Americans, miniature portraits were often painted on ivory. Still in its original case, this miniature of William Aiken Jr. (1806–1887) was painted during a visit to France. The art of miniature painting all but disappeared with the advent of daguerreotype photography in the 1840s.

> *Last night I was at the handsomest ball I have ever seen—given by Mrs. Aiken, Miss Lowndes that was—they live near Boundary Street in a house he has added to, & furnished very handsomely—2 floors were entirely thrown open—the orchestra from the theatre played for the dances—and the supper table was covered with a rich service of silver—light in profusion, & a crowded handsomely draped assembly—M & E enjoyed themselves very much—though they are not among the waltzers—consequently have to sit still, whenever that dance which is a favorite with those who call themselves the fashionables is called for.*[31]

While this event was the "handsomest ball" that the narrator had ever seen, it seems unlikely that it was a singular event for the Aikens.

During the first few years of life in the house, the Aikens focused on lavishly decorating in the most current fashion and caring for their first child, Henrietta, born in July 1836. A son

named Thomas was born in 1841, and he shortly thereafter died, leaving Henrietta as the Aikens' only child. During this time, William Aiken launched a political career. In 1838, he was elected to the first of three successive terms in the South Carolina legislature, followed by his election as governor in 1844. Service to the state required an investment of time in Columbia, but Aiken's extensive business interests and the requirements of political life ensured a steady schedule of entertaining at their Charleston residence.

Further Expansion by William and Harriet Aiken, 1857–1858

For William and Harriet Aiken, the 1850s marked a continuation of the public and social life that they had enjoyed since moving to Elizabeth Street. Aiken was elected to Congress as a South Carolina representative in 1851 and served until 1857. After completing his third term, he returned to Charleston, and in August 1857 the Aikens, with their daughter Henrietta, departed by steamer for New York on the first leg of a European grand tour. Their acquisition of art and sculpture on that trip was significant, for the voyage coincided with a new construction project at home.

The house again underwent major structural changes. Both staircases were upgraded and the back staircase was improved to allow better access to the second and third floors. Two bedchambers were added to the third story. Dressing rooms were also built for the large, south-facing bedchambers on that floor. Given the small size of the Aiken family, the number of sleeping quarters suggests an active social life with frequent overnight guests.

The renovation project also included the construction of a new wing on the northwest corner of the house. The one-story addition was designed to serve as an art gallery. Located adjacent to the elaborate west entrance, the gallery wing provided architectural balance to the Elizabeth Street side of the house as well as an elegant room in which to display the family's collection of art and sculpture. Cousin and artist Joseph Daniel Aiken oversaw the construction of the art gallery. Having received drawings for the room while in Paris, the Aikens purchased copies of old masters, sculptures, and objects d'art to decorate the gallery during their journey across Europe. The scaled plan drawings of the art gallery and the first-floor rooms of the main block, which are among the Aiken family papers at The Charleston Museum, include room designations, the locations of fireplaces and gaslight fixtures, and detailed dimensions of almost every wall surface, as well as a height dimension for the double drawing rooms. Considering that the dimensions are given to the half inch, it seems these renderings were produced after the rooms were completed and were intended to assist the Aikens in planning the placement of their newly acquired paintings and sculpture.

The designation of gas fixtures on the plans highlights another aspect of the 1857–58 renovation: Charleston was among the first cities in the country to develop a municipal gas system, and by the mid-1850s piped gas was available in the more prosperous parts of the city. While a municipal water system was slower to develop, improvements in plumbing using onsite cisterns in place of a citywide supply of water were increasingly accessible. The desire for gas lighting and modern plumbing combined with new decorative fashions drove many wealthy urban homeowners to renovate and upgrade their houses, and this trend is well documented in Charleston. By the mid- to late 1850s, scores of upscale Charleston houses, including the Nathaniel Russell House, were fitted with gas lighting, interior water closets, and bathing fixtures. At the Aiken-Rhett House, lighting and plumbing improvements were combined with the installation of a service-bell system and updated decorative schemes to again modernize the house in the latest fashion.

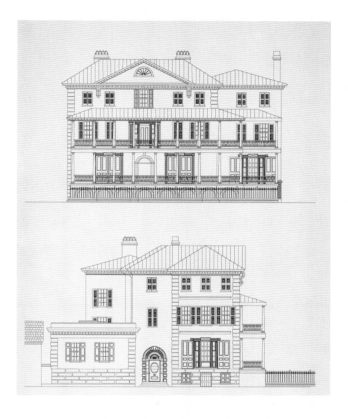

South and west elevations, circa 1858.

The addition of a one-story art gallery on the Elizabeth Street side of the house was part of the final phase of the Aikens' 1858 renovation. When viewing the main entrance, the five-hundred-square-foot gallery wing reestablishes a sense of balance to the western side of the house.

The Civil War, 1861–1865

The Civil War years were a turbulent time for the Aiken family as they watched great change and experienced much loss. Aiken was a Unionist and opposed the war, so it must have been disconcerting when their only child, Henrietta, married Andrew Burnet Rhett, son of Robert Barnwell Rhett, one of the South's most outspoken secessionists. Their union joined two prominent but politically polar South Carolina families.

The Aikens may not have wholly approved of their daughter's suitor. In a passionate letter composed in the winter of 1861 urging her to accept his marriage proposal, Rhett wrote to Henrietta Aiken, "You may sacrifice me now because you are unwilling to bear the annoyances of your sick pacified Father any longer." Rhett went on to predict that "parental tyranny" would bring her "anguish and misery." He wrote:

You offer to give me a decided final answer in June. Etta the issue is too great, greater than I can bear. I have no great fear of death but the [thought] of life without you suddenly appalls me. Life without you would be a burden and a curse to me. You have become so entwined with my thoughts, and associated with things without that at every turn in life the recollection of you would meet and overwhelm me, until like Job's wife I should "curse God and die!"[32]

1865 stereoscopic view of exterior.
The earliest known image of the Aiken-Rhett House, this photograph was taken in 1865 and was distributed nationally as a stereograph. A study of its details reveals several features no longer extant, such as a *chevaux-de-frise* mounted vertically on the Elizabeth Street side column, a parapet installed on the piazza roof, and Wickersham fencing around Wragg Square. *Photograph courtesy of the Library of Congress, LC-DIG-cwpb-03021.*

Amidst a terrible lightning storm while on furlough from the war, Andrew Burnet Rhett married "the greatest heiress in the state, Miss Aiken."[33] The wedding took place at the Aikens' house in Flat Rock, North Carolina, on August 21, 1862. For the occasion, Rhett requested that his brother, Edmund, have a new coat made for him and instructed him to:

[T]ell the person who is to make it that it is for my wedding coat and that it must be <u>lined throughout</u> with <u>white silk</u>…the facings will be Artillery (scarlet cloth)…and get a handsome shade of blue-grey. If either tailor [sic] has any white casimere [sic] I should like to have a pair of white cassimere pants with a scarlet cord down the side and a plain white silk military vest.[34]

The bride's attire for the wedding is unknown, and in contrast to Rhett, who commissioned fine clothing from a tailor, her bridesmaid, Julia Rutledge, made her gown from curtain material that she had purchased before the war. Rhett presented Henrietta with a ring engraved, "A.B. Rhett to H.A. Aiken Augt. 21st 1862."[35]

Despite familial ties and his love of home, William Aiken Jr. was a staunch Unionist and remained so throughout the war. In an 1865 letter published in the *New York Times*, Aiken wrote with great sorrow, "I am pecuniarily [*sic*] almost ruined, as well as all of us here; but thank God I am clear of the blood that has been shed. If my advice had been taken war never would have raised its head in this great and glorious republic; but evil counsels were allowed to prevail."[36]

Contemporary accounts suggest that William Aiken Jr. had the dubious distinction of being imprisoned twice—once by the Confederacy and once by the United States government. In 1863, Parson W.G. Brownlow reported in the *New York Times* that Aiken was detained in Richmond's Libby Prison for refusing to take an oath of allegiance to the Confederacy. Brownlow pleaded for his release, and stated, "He is a Union man, and stubbornly refuses to be anything else…His cruel confinement has been kept a secret from the outside world, and it has been kept out of Southern papers, because his villainous persecutors were ashamed to let his imprisonment be known."[37] Then, in 1865, Governor Aiken was reputedly arrested by Federal troops for not attending the raising of the American flag at a ceremony at Fort Sumter. Taken to Washington for trial, Aiken was released following the intervention of several prominent Northern political leaders and President Andrew Johnson, whom he had befriended while a member of Congress.

Regardless of Aiken's political leanings and resulting difficulties, several notable Confederates visited Aiken's house during the war. In November 1863, Confederate President Jefferson Davis visited Charleston and stayed one week at the Aiken-Rhett House. Brigadier General Pierre Gustave Toutant Beauregard moved his headquarters into the house in December 1864 to escape the heavy Federal bombardment of the city. When Charleston fell to the advancing Union armies, both the Aikens' city house and plantation, Jehossee, were extensively looted.

After the Civil War, Aiken was again elected to the United States House of Representatives but was denied his seat in the political controversy surrounding Reconstruction. One of Aiken's last positions

The Peabody Fund Commission.
In 1867, George Peabody invited William Aiken Jr. to serve on the Peabody Fund Commission. The fund was established to address the lack of educational opportunities for children in the South after the Civil War. Serving on the committee were some of America's most influential men of the era, both Northerners and Southerners. *Standing, left to right*: Admiral David G. Farragut; Honorable Hamilton Fish of New York; General Ulysses S. Grant; Governor William Aiken Jr.; Episcopal Bishop Charles P. McIlvane of Ohio; and George B. Westmore of Rhode Island. *Seated, left to right*: George Peabody; J.P. Chase; and Honorable Robert Winthrop of Massachusetts. *Photograph courtesy of the National Archives.*

of public service was as a trustee of the Peabody Fund to promote education in the war-torn South.

An Elegant Retirement, 1865–1892

In the late nineteenth and early twentieth centuries, as the Aiken family grew and fashions changed, the Aikens updated the interiors of their house. These alterations served to spruce up the rooms rather than significantly alter its historic fabric. Family records indicate that in 1874 several decorative improvements were made throughout the house. In December 1874, Aiken updated and cleaned window dressings and purchased new bedroom furniture, probably for the third floor, from Millings & Livingston of Charleston. Invoices indicate that the Aikens hung pictures in different locations, moved sculptures, and lined several photographs.[38]

Henrietta Aiken Rhett, whose own family continued to live in the house, worked closely with her parents to complete these projects. In fact, many of the alterations most certainly related to her marriage to Andrew Burnet Rhett in 1862 and the steady increase of their family. A.B. Rhett served in the Confederate army, achieved the rank of major, and survived the war. By 1870, Andrew and Henrietta Rhett were living with the Aikens on Elizabeth Street. Their first of five children, William Aiken Rhett, was born on May 1, 1869. The southwest bedchamber and dressing room on the third floor were modified to permit direct access from the center passage to the dressing room. Probably at this time a stove flue was cut in to provide heat to the dressing room. These changes are just what might be expected to occur along with the birth of Henrietta Aiken Rhett's first child—conversion of an unheated dressing room to a heated chamber in proximity to the mother.

Their second child, Edmund Rhett, was born in January 1871 and the third, Harriet Lowndes Rhett, in May 1872. The Rhett family continued to grow with the births of I'On Lowndes Rhett in November 1876 and Andrew Burnet Rhett Jr. in November 1877. Between the arrivals of the last two children, the house was repainted, most likely for the first time since the Civil War. Shades of yellow, burnt umber, and "Imperial Scarlet" were used and remnants of these colors can be seen throughout the house today.

A likely division of living space in the house would have placed William and Harriet Aiken on the second floor of the main house with A.B. and Henrietta Rhett and their children on the

Henrietta Aiken Rhett.
The only surviving child of William and Harriett Aiken Jr., Henrietta Aiken was born in July 1836. She married Andrew Burnet Rhett in Flat Rock, North Carolina, in 1862. Together they raised five children in the Aiken-Rhett House: William (1869–1932), Edmund (1871–1931), Harriet (1872–1935), I'On (1876–1959) and Andrew Burnet Jr. (1877–1946). Henrietta Rhett died on December 14, 1918, at the age of eighty-two.

third story. Tragedy struck the Rhett family on September 13, 1879, when Andrew Burnet Rhett died at the age of forty-five. His widow and their five young children, ranging from twenty-two months to ten years of age, remained in the house with the Aikens.

With three generations of the Aiken and Rhett families living in the house throughout the late nineteenth century, most bedchambers were occupied by family members, leaving limited room for short-term guests. However, at various times 48 Elizabeth Street served as home for other family members. The city directory for 1866 lists B. S. Rhett as a resident, evidently referring to Benjamin S. Rhett, uncle of Andrew Burnet Rhett. The directory for 1875–76 lists Barnwell Rhett as a member of the household, presumably a reference to A.B. Rhett's brother, who was at the time editor of the *Journal of Commerce*. Governor Aiken wrote to his cousin Joseph D. Aiken on December 11, 1885: "Your mother and sister having returned to the City, are most comfortably lodged here for the winter."[39] It was indeed a full house; the Aikens loved to entertain and welcomed guests and family alike.

On September 6, 1887, Governor William Aiken Jr. died at the family home in Flat Rock, leaving his wife and daughter as his sole heirs. His obituary recorded that "he was not made of the stern stuff of which the rulers of mankind are composed. More than this, he was honorable, useful, loyal, in every public relation, and in every private sphere as well."[40]

Harriet Lowndes Aiken remained the matriarch of the family, and she shared her house with her daughter and grandchildren as well as various other extended members of the family. Henrietta Aiken Rhett's oldest child, William, was eighteen and her youngest was ten at the time of their grandfather's death. Harriet Aiken converted the large second-floor drawing room into her bedchamber and the remaining family occupied the adjacent bedrooms and upstairs compartments.

On March 24, 1892, Harriet Lowndes Aiken died in Charleston at the age of eighty, leaving her widowed daughter as her only heir. At the age of fifty-five, Henrietta Aiken Rhett assumed sole ownership of her parents' house.

Andrew Burnet Rhett.

Photographed in his uniform, Andrew Burnet Rhett served in the Confederate forces as an artillery officer, eventually obtaining the rank of major. The son of staunch secessionist, or fire-eater, Robert Barnwell Rhett, Andrew survived the Civil War and died in Flat Rock, North Carolina, in 1879.

Henrietta Aiken Rhett, 1892–1918

The Aiken-Rhett House remained the center of family life for Henrietta, even as her children moved away for college, married, and had families of their own. She also began to entertain on a scale that was only slightly less splendid than before the war. Throughout the last quarter of the nineteenth century, the family also persisted in their improvements to the house and grounds.

Henrietta Rhett's daughter Harriet's debut may have inspired her to again paint the house and redecorate—which most often meant moving the family heirlooms to another location. She paid a hefty sum of $123.37 to A. O'Connell, "Painter and Dealer in Paints," of 84 Meeting Street.[41] Shortly thereafter, she hosted a magnificent affair to introduce her daughter into society. She wrote her son Edmund Rhett:

> *We have issued five hundred invitations and the amount of money it is involving is frightful…I hope I may get the direct tax money for I count on it to defray the expense of painting, carpets, ect. And Sissy's outfit as a "Society Girl" together with the other heavy expenses I have to meet during the winter.[42]*

Piazza.

One of the main architectural characteristics of Charleston houses is the porch, or piazza. The first-floor piazza of the Aiken-Rhett House is accessed through the large, triple-hung sash windows that were installed in the 1830s, replacing the comparatively small Robinson-era nine-over-nine window sashes.

Harriet Rhett was the first of Henrietta Rhett's five children to marry in 1896, followed by William Rhett in 1901 and Edmund Rhett in 1902. I'On Rhett did not marry until 1932, and the youngest son, Andrew Burnet Rhett Jr., remained a bachelor until his death in 1946. The youngest two children lived in the Aiken-Rhett House for the remainder of their lives.

An Extended Family Residence, 1918–1946

On December 14, 1918, Henrietta Aiken Rhett died at the age of eighty-two, leaving her five children as heirs. At the time of her death, the family photographed the double parlors, capturing on film the rooms as they had been furnished for several decades. Many of the decorative objects and furnishings in the house were then divided among the five children. For the next half-dozen years, the core of the household continued to be William Rhett, his wife and daughter, and bachelor brothers I'On Rhett and Andrew Burnet Rhett Jr. Structurally, few changes occurred to the property, with the exception of minor decorative trimmings and a kitchen addition to the rear of the house.

A family letter, dated February 6, 1925, confirmed that William Rhett had moved and suggests that a sale of the property of the house was at least rumored, and most likely was considered and rejected by his brothers. A relative from New York corresponded with Andrew Burnet Rhett Jr.:

Someone wrote months ago that your dear old home, 48 Elizabeth St. had been sold, & that [William] *Aiken was in his house on South Bay, but did not write where you & I'On were. I suppose it was a mistake & the house is <u>not</u> sold; I certainly like to think of you and I'On still being there & hope you don't feel too lonely. I am so much attached to the old house with its thousands of associations with my long past, that I can truly sympathize with all of you in hating to give it up.*[43]

Back view of the house.

The rear view of the Aiken-Rhett House clearly shows its evolution from a balanced and symmetrical Charleston double house to the greatly expanded, asymmetrical Greek Revival mansion. The original structure, center right, was more than doubled in size by the addition of the east wing and art gallery.

From 1927 until 1932, I'On Rhett and Andrew Burnet Rhett Jr. were the only family members listed as living in the house. They had purchased their siblings' shares of the property and together were determined to preserve their grandparents' formerly grand antebellum mansion. In July 1932, at the age of fifty-five, I'On Rhett married Frances Hinson Dill. The couple shared the Aiken-Rhett

House and, evidently, the cost of its maintenance, with Andrew Burnet Rhett Jr. until his death in 1946 at the age of sixty-eight.

I'On and Frances Rhett, 1946–1975

After Andrew Burnet Rhett Jr.'s death, and for the first time since 1836, the house was occupied by a single generation of the family—a married couple unencumbered by siblings and other relations. For the next decade, I'On and Frances Rhett maintained the house with heirloom furnishings and art scattered among the various rooms, many of which remained closed to family and visitors alike. The couple enjoyed their tenure for only a little more than a decade. On December 18, 1959, I'On Rhett died at the age of eighty-three, leaving Frances Dill Rhett as his sole heir. She continued to live in the house by herself for some years, but by 1968 the house had become vacant after she moved to 19 Legare Street with her sister Pauline Dill. Family members recall that Frances Rhett lived in just a few rooms of the house after her husband's death, and upon her departure the house was simply closed up with furnishings still in place—a condition that continued until 1975.

The dining room in 1958.

Historic American Buildings photographer Louis I. Schwartz captured the dining room during I'On and Frances Dill Rhett's tenure. The room was decorated with family heirlooms inherited by the couple, and many of these objects, including the exquisite sideboard with marble columns, dining table, chairs, and center table, remain on view at the Aiken-Rhett House. *Photograph courtesy of the Library of Congress.*

A Historic House Becomes a Historic House Museum

Aware of the historical significance of The Aiken-Rhett House and concerned with its future, Frances Dill Rhett donated the property to The Charleston Museum in 1975. There were concerns about the financial burden to the museum, yet almost universally Charlestonians voiced a determination to preserve the property. Opening the house as a museum was not immediate or permanent. The first public viewing of the house was for only three weeks in the spring of 1979.

Initially, The Charleston Museum intended to completely restore the structure; however, paying for the restoration was a challenge. Numerous fundraising events, such as a Haunted House Tour and periodic short-term openings, generated money for various projects during the late 1970s and early 1980s. The rental of the property as a photography location, for both print and film, was another method to raise much-needed funds for the restoration and conservation of the house and its collection, which was initially composed of family artifacts inherited by I'On Rhett and transferred to the museum by Francis Dill Rhett. In 1985, the Aiken-Rhett House was featured in *Architectural Digest*. Portions of the cult film *Swamp Thing* were filmed in the house in 1981, as was a made-for-television movie, *A Special Friendship*, in 1986.

The Charleston Museum's interpretive strategy for the house was novel. The decision was made, not without internal debate, to conserve and protect the original historic fabric on the first floor rather than restore it to a conjectural interior. At the same time, plans were proposed, but not carried out, to use the second floor of the Aiken-Rhett as exhibition space for the museum's nineteenth-century decorative arts collection. Eventually, the museum determined to preserve all of the building interiors in their current state, which was a precedent established by the National Trust at Drayton Hall, but unique on the Charleston peninsula.

Newspaper accounts during the 1990s documented The Charleston Museum's growing fiscal challenges as it continued to own and operate the Aiken-Rhett as a historic site. Repairs from Hurricane Hugo had only added to the financial burden. With the possibility of the house going for sale on the open market, proponents of preserving the property as a museum convinced the board of trustees of Historic Charleston Foundation to purchase the site.

When Historic Charleston Foundation assumed ownership of the Aiken-Rhett House in 1995, a panel of national preservation experts helped arrive at the decision to preserve the structure rather than attempt to restore it to a particular period in its history. The one exception was a restoration of the art gallery, which had suffered extensive water damage and the removal of a cinderblock kitchen that had been built between the main house and east dependency in the 1950s. A major accomplishment in the long-term preservation of the property was the completion of a two-volume Historic Structures Report (HSR) in 2004 by architectural historians Orlando Ridout V, Willie Graham, and Carl Lounsbury. The report was an in-depth history of the site's buildings, down to the pattern of molding in each room. The HSR was a critical component in planning the 2007–08 exterior restoration of the main house as part of a Save America's Treasures (SAT) Grant.

The natural decay of the building's exterior components in Charleston's harsh climate had reached a point where water was migrating into the interior. With the goal of sealing the building's envelope, the exterior restoration returned the house to its 1858 appearance based on physical evidence studied by paint conservator Susan Buck. The result is a unique approach in HCF's stewardship of the house. While the SAT grant work restored and protected the building's exterior, its original historic interior will continue to be stabilized and conserved.

The west parlor in 1990.
During The Charleston Museum's tenure, the museum exhibited portions of its nineteenth-century decorative art collection throughout the Aiken-Rhett House. The late nineteenth-century window treatments pictured in the Rhett family's 1918 photograph remained on view, as evidenced by John McWilliams's Historic American Buildings Survey photograph. *Photograph courtesy of the Library of Congress, HABS SC, 10-CHAR, 177-65.*

The Entry Hall

Upon approaching the front entrance of the Aiken-Rhett House, visitors immediately encounter the mahogany door and its ornate surround. Contemporary pattern books, such as Minard Lafever's 1829 *The Young Builders General Instructor*, most likely informed the Aiken-Rhett doorway, and an almost identical design surrounds the front door of the Merchant's House (circa 1832) Museum in New York. Passing through the entrance, it is clear that the Aiken-Rhett's formal entry hall was intended to inspire awe. The entrance was moved to the Elizabeth Street façade of the house circa 1835, and the entry hall with its elegant double staircase and vaulted ceiling reinforced the Aikens' social aspirations.

The grand sweep of the matched pair of curving staircases is striking. Embellished with mahogany handrails and cast-iron balustrade, the double staircase is made of cantilevered marble steps. The vaulted ceiling displays Greek Revival decorative designs, such as Greek key meanders and acanthus leaves, which illustrate the shift away from the delicate, restrained late Federal style of John Robinson's era to the bolder and more derivative late classical period.

Unfortunately, none of the original nineteenth-century paint scheme of the entry hall remains visible, but evidence of its rich hues is preserved underneath the subsequent layers. Paint conservator Susan Buck studied the Aiken-Rhett House for more than ten years

Entry hall.

Cantilevered marble steps, fluted columns, cast-iron railings with classically inspired anthemion detailing, a gracefully curved mahogany handrail, and the double staircase made an imposing and elegant entrance to the Aikens' renovated mansion. The ribs and medallion on the vaulted ceiling and details in the bold Greek Revival–style molding were originally gilded. The wall surfaces seen today are the result of a 1980s renovation, which does not accurately reflect the grandeur of the original decorative scheme.

and her research uncovered that in the nineteenth century the walls and ceilings were simply brilliant in appearance, with a blue ceiling and gilt center medallion and ribbing.

The Double Parlors

When the entry hall was constructed, the first floor was reconfigured by the Aikens to include a library, dining room, and double parlors. Originally designed as four rooms separated into pairs by a central hallway, the new floor plan included two larger, grander public rooms, which extended across the south side of the house with large windows opening onto the piazza. Sliding, mahogany veneered pocket doors made it possible to separate the rooms, or when opened, use them as a single grand entertaining suite. Governor Aiken's social and political prominence meant that the family entertained frequently and grandly. Frederika Bremer recalled that almost five hundred people were invited to a party she attended at the house in the 1850s:

> *I have, besides, been to a great entertainment given by the Governor of South Carolina, Mr. Akin [sic], and his lovely wife. There was very beautiful music; and for the rest, conversation in the room, or out under the piazzas, in the shade of blossoming creepers, the clematis, the caprifolium [sic], and roses, quite romantic in the soft night air. Five hundred persons, it is said, were invited, and the entertainment was one of the most beautiful I have been present at in this country.* [44]

During such events, guests would have had accessed the first-floor piazza through the triple-hung windows in the parlor or the dining room.

Music was a particular interest of the Aiken family, and Henrietta Rhett's piano remains in its original place in the double parlors. In the nineteenth century, learning to play an instrument was an important aspect of a young woman's education. Henrietta Rhett's piano in the east parlor was purchased by her mother from

Surviving decorative elements.
The gold-leaf curtain rod finials seen here are visible in the 1918 photograph of the west parlor.

West parlor, 1918.
This view of the west parlor captures vestiges of the textiles that decorated the space in the Victorian era. Furniture purchased during the antebellum period, such as the pair of armchairs attributed to Duncan Phyfe and a card table made by Deming and Bulkley, still adorn the parlor today. *Photograph courtesy of The Charleston Museum.*

West parlor today.

All objects in the Aiken-Rhett House collection were originally owned by the Robinson and Aiken-Rhett families, and many of the items are still in the rooms for which they were purchased. Through acquisition as well as the generosity of donors, artifacts related to the Aiken-Rhett and Robinson families continue to return to 48 Elizabeth Street.

the Chickering Piano Company following the Civil War. Harriet Aiken's niece, Mary Huger Cottenet, sold one of her aunt's rings in New York to generate money for the purchase. Writing to her aunt about the matter, Mary laments:

> *It pains me, dear Aunt Heart…to dispose of your ring, but of course you have thought it over well & made up your mind. I am glad however that there is a prospect of Etta's* [Harriet's daughter, Henrietta] *using her fine voice again & hope that next Winter you will invite me to some of the musical reunions you are contemplating.*[45]

In addition to the piano, at least two pieces of music directly associated with the Aikens survive. Marie R. Siegling composed and dedicated a piece of pianoforte music, titled "Souvenir de Charleston," to Harriet Aiken in 1846. "Governor Aiken's March," also for the pianoforte, was arranged in his honor by William Herwig in 1845. Such sheet music would have been kept in the family's mahogany canterbury.

CANTERBURY, **probably New York, early nineteenth century. Mahogany. Gift of Mrs. Frances Dill Rhett through transfer from The Charleston Museum to Historic Charleston Foundation, 96.3.23.**

Canterburys were stands with divisions used for holding sheet music and sometimes newspaper and magazines. This example is almost identical to one Duncan Phyfe made for his daughter, Eliza Vail, which is illustrated in Nancy McClelland's *Duncan Phyfe and the English Regency*.

PROSERPINE, **circa 1840, by Hiram Powers (1805–1873, American). Marble. Gift to Historic Charleston Foundation through transfer from The Charleston Museum, 96.3.45.**

Powers was a famed American sculptor who settled in Florence in 1837 and remained in Italy for the rest of his life. His studio was among the popular grand tour stops. Harriet Aiken wrote in her travel diary on November 17, 1857, from Florence that she had "commissioned a sculpture from Powers." *Proserpine* was among his most popular sculptures. He created almost two hundred of the busts in varying sizes during his career.

Detail of plaster ceiling medallion.

Throughout the nineteenth century, the Aikens continued to redecorate their house. While this parlor ceiling medallion was most likely installed in the 1830s, paint analysis dates the visible gilding to the 1870s.

Wallpaper panel.

The intact panel of decorative wallpaper is most probably of French manufacture and dates to the 1850s renovation.

East parlor, 1918.

This photograph of the east parlor shows three of the marble statues now exhibited in the art gallery. The statue on the far left is a copy of Canova's *Venus Italica*, which was loosely copied after the Medici *Venus*. Charlestonians recorded much commentary and often made comparisons between the two Venuses in their travel diaries and letters home. *Photograph courtesy of The Charleston Museum.*

East parlor today.

Created during the 1830s renovations by the removal of the original central hall, the double parlors are divided by two mahogany-veneered pocket doors. The matching chandeliers in the parlors are believed to have been purchased abroad. Flagg's grand portrait of Harriet Aiken was originally in the art gallery and was moved in front of the window during the twentieth century.

The Library

Libraries were the epitome of refinement in the nineteenth-century house, and it was fashionable to collect volumes of books, which expressed one's sophistication and learnedness. The Aiken family was well educated, spoke several languages, and traveled extensively. Including almost two thousand extant volumes, the library collection offers insight into their interests and covers a wide range of subject matter, including histories, popular novels of the day, etiquette manuals, religious texts, and travel guides. Many volumes in the collection were signed by family members and inscribed with the date and place of purchase. Classical literature in the collection, required reading for the social elite in antebellum Charleston, includes the works of Shakespeare, Voltaire, Fontaine, and Sir Walter Scott. Poetry was also a topic of choice for the Aikens, with multivolume sets of Milton, Alexander Pope, and Lord Byron.

The library room itself is not large enough to house the entire two thousand volumes, despite the built-in bookcases, which are faced in mahogany, and the books would have been displayed in bookcases throughout the house. A unique mahogany table with an extremely wide base rests in the center of the room. Originally it may have been custom built to keep oversized folios, but by the twentieth century the family had come to refer to it as Uncle I'On's "hat table."

Library.

More than two thousand volumes remain of the Aiken family's book collection. Avid readers, the Aikens purchased many books during their travels, both domestically and abroad. The collection contains guidebooks and travel guides, as well as popular fiction and religious and political treatises, both contemporary and classical. Many bear the inscription of the family member who originally owned the book.

The Dining Room

The east wing of the Aiken-Rhett House was added in the early 1830s and consists of a warming kitchen on the ground floor and a dining room on the first. Elaborate dinner parties and balls characterized Charleston's social season, and the addition of a large dining room with a ground-floor staging area for food preparation reinforces the notion that the Aikens renovated the house to accommodate large entertainments. Guest lists, bills for the purchase of food, and firsthand accounts give insight into events at 48 Elizabeth Street, particularly during the years when William Aiken was politically active.

During Confederate President Jefferson Davis's visit to Charleston in November of 1863, William Aiken, who was on the Arrangements Committee, hosted a dinner for the city's civic and military leaders. Although women were not present at this dinner, diarist Mary Boykin Chesnut provided a brief account of this occasion in her memoirs:

> *Mr. Davis visited Charleston and had an enthusiastic reception, Beauregard, Rhetts, Jordans to the contrary notwithstanding. He described it all to Mr. Preston. Mr. Aiken's perfect old Carolina style of living delighted him; those old gray-haired darkies and their automatic, noiseless perfection of training. One does miss that sort of thing. Your own servants think for you, they even know your ways and your wants, they save you all responsibility even in matters of your own ease and well-being.* [46]

Her description reveals how reliant slave owners were on their enslaved servants during important social events. Slaves were instrumental in the preparation and execution of the grand affairs that garnered their owners' social status and recognition.

The Aikens' New York–made mahogany dining table was used during family dinners, and it extended to seat twenty-two people during larger functions. A pair of marble-top sideboards, of which one remains in the house, was used to lavishly display the Aikens' silver. According to an account given by Governor Aiken to Nathaniel Bishop, the Aikens owned approximately $45,000 worth of silver, a significant portion of which was inherited. This valuable collection was hidden during the war at their family plantation Jehossee and eventually "went to enrich the spoils of the Union

SAUCE TUREEN WITH COVER AND STAND, **Worcester, England, circa 1813, by Flight, Barr and Barr (partnership dates, 1813–1829). Porcelain with polychrome enamel. Gift of the heirs of Mary Green Maybank, 2003.3.30.**
SAUCE LADLE, **New York, 1876. Silver, engraved with the initials "HR" for Henrietta Rhett. Gift of the Mary Green Maybank heirs, 2000.3.11.**

In the "Japan" pattern, this sauce tureen is part of a larger dinnerware set owned by Thomas Lowndes, father of Harriet Lowndes Aiken. The set descended in the Aiken-Rhett family.

Dining room.

Grand dinner parties were one of the most popular entertainments and important social events, particularly for a politician such as William Aiken. The Aikens hosted numerous distinguished guests, including President of the Confederacy Jefferson Davis and internationally renowned, nineteenth-century Swedish author Frederika Bremer.

army" when the property was looted.[47] The sideboards would have indeed been impressive sites with such a profusion of silver adorning their surfaces.

A mirror, also original to the house, still hangs above the mantel. In the center of the room an Argand chandelier, circa 1830, extends from the exquisite plaster ceiling medallion.

Hurricane Hugo's damage to the property in 1989 is evident in the dining room. After several of the chimneys were blown down, water penetrated the roof and damaged the plaster cornice. The Charleston Museum, owner of the property at the time, made the interpretive decision to leave all hurricane repairs in the plaster's natural, bright white so that they are easily discernable. Despite the removal of wallpaper in the room, the decision not to restore the walls preserved the shadows or ghosts of early wall coverings.

The Art Gallery

In 1857, while the Aikens were on their final grand tour before the Civil War, a second period of renovation took place. During this phase, the house's interior was redecorated and infrastructure improvements, such as the installation of gas lighting, were made. The last major alteration to the house was the construction of the art gallery. While in Europe, Governor Aiken's cousin Joseph Daniel Aiken sent him a scale drawing of the room so that appropriately sized artwork could be purchased.

The Aikens' itinerary included extensive travel in England, France, Germany, Czechoslovakia, and Austria, followed by a prolonged tour of Italy. Their progress can be tracked by entries in Harriet Aiken's travel diary. The Aikens were following a grand tradition of European travel by wealthy Americans, and it is most likely no coincidence

FISH SLICE AND FORK SET, **New York, patented 1847, by William Gale and Son (1850–1866). Silver, engraved with the initials "HR" for Henrietta Rhett. Gift of the Mary Green Maybank heirs, 2000.3.17.**

The Aikens adorned their interiors with the finest silver and porcelains. Among the extant items is this rare Gothic-pattern fish slice and fork in the original box. It is no coincidence that the family chose decorative objects that closely relate to the Gothic elements found on the property's outbuildings.

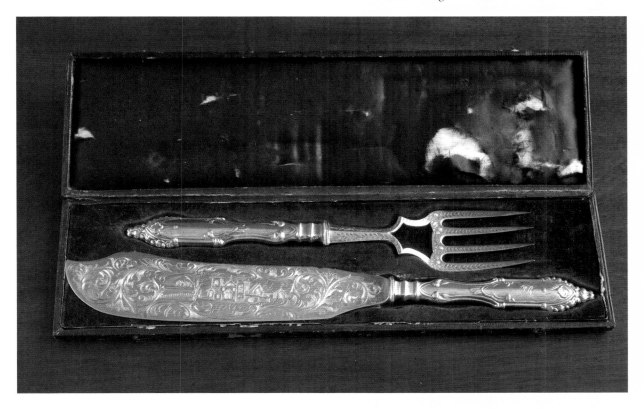

Art gallery.

While the Aikens were traveling abroad, cousin and artist Joseph Daniel Aiken (1817–1884) oversaw the construction of the art gallery. He sent a drawing and measurements for the room to the Aikens in Paris. William and Harriet Aiken purchased copies of old masters, sculptures, and objects d'art during their journey across Europe.

that their daughter was twenty-one years old and unmarried when they departed. The trip would have served as an opportunity for the elder Aikens to enrich their own appreciation for European art, architecture, and social conventions while also introducing their daughter to an elevated level of society.

At the beginning of their travels, Harriet reported that the group had arrived in Paris "with a ridiculous quantity of Trunks—distributed in three Carriages." Their load was only increased as they proceeded through Europe, making purchases along the way that were eventually shipped to Charleston. She recorded that they bought "some pictures" in Rome and two statues in Florence, one of which was the sculpture *Proserpine* by the famed Hiram Powers.[48]

The walls of the art gallery were crowded during the nineteenth century, with more than thirty

paintings exhibited. Most of the fine art and sculptures were copies after the old masters or reflected the sentimental tastes of the day. Exhibited in the center of the room is a sculpture of Mary Magdalene, whose left hand rests on a copy of the Old and New Testaments. After the original by Pampaloni, Italian sculptor D. Menconi inscribed "Firenze 1858" on the statue. Other sculptures exhibited in the art gallery include a copy of Antonio Canova's *Venus Italica* and the *Shepherd Boy* by E.S. Bartholemew. Interestingly, copying other objects of art was an extremely popular practice in the late nineteenth century and was not considered plagiarism.

The objects in the Aikens' gallery represent all that the grand tour encompassed: refinement, intellectual pursuits, and connections with "the old country." A newspaper description of the room in the late nineteenth century stated:

In studying the pictures owned by Mrs. Gov. Aiken, full scope is allowed for diversity of taste, as here one finds the mellowed tints and hues softened by the hand of time…Here also are a number of beautiful specimens of the sculptor's art ranged about in niches and corners of the handsomely constructed mansion…A life size portrait of Mrs. Aiken by George Whiting Flagg, occupies a large canvas, over which, when not exposed to view hangs a heavy crimson curtain…L. Terry's "Romeo and Juliet"…a Bandit scene by Salvator Rosa…A village scene supposed to be by David Teniers…three Strolling Musicians…The Flight into Egypt…In sculpture the choicest piece…is an exquisitely modeled bust of Proserpine by Hiram Powers…other works in marble comprise a life size reclining Magdalene, a fine reproduction of Canova's Venus of the Bath, a Shepherd Boy, and The First Grief.[49]

The art gallery's skylight dates to 1858 and provides natural, diffused light with which to view the artworks. The Aiken-Rhett family continued to use the art gallery in the twentieth century. It became a center for family social life and, once a year, Mr. and Mrs. I'On Rhett hosted a Christmas party there for fellow Aiken descendants.

ROMEO AND JULIET, **circa 1857, by Luther Terry (1813–1900, American expatriate artist in Rome, Italy). Oil on canvas. Gift of Mr. and Mrs. Joseph Maybank through transfer from The Charleston Museum to Historic Charleston Foundation, 96.3.5. Back is labeled: "Please Do Not Touch For 24 Hours/Still Wet."**

Harriet Aiken refers to her visit to Juliet's tomb in her 1857 travel diary. As with so many other paintings, it is thought that this work was purchased during the Aikens' 1857–58 grand tour. Luther Terry was an American expatriate who lived in Rome, and he was known to have executed several paintings based on subjects from Shakespearean works.

The Second Floor Hallway

Once on the second floor, the main architectural feature of the hall is the arch that separates the staircase from the hallway. The carved keystone in the center of the arch and the supporting columns of fluted, intricate gouge work combine to form a visually intriguing frame for the passageway. A small pulley, mounted at the base of the keystone, served as a mechanism to allow the house slaves to lower and service a chandelier that once hung from the stair hall ceiling.

Two brass gaslight fixtures flank the elliptical arch. One fixture was electrified in the early twentieth century while the other retains its gas fittings and glass globes, perhaps due to the notorious unreliability of early electrical service. The width of the hall and height of the ceiling were the result of both form and function. The hall retains its Federal-era proportions, a product of which allowed for air circulation throughout the house. Hallways served as ancillary rooms where one could sit to enjoy the breeze and, therefore, the second-floor passage was furnished.

The Bedchambers

Although bedrooms are considered to be private spaces today, that was not the case in the nineteenth-century house. Bedchambers, while primarily a place for sleeping, were in many ways multipurpose rooms. In addition to beds, bedchambers were also furnished with

Stair hall.
The contrast between the bold Greek Revival architectural details on the first floor and the comparatively understated Federal-style elements on the second is striking. The stair hall is a transitional space between the two, as few architectural changes were made during the Aikens' renovations.

sofas, chairs, and tables. Numerous nineteenth-century accounts reveal that bedchambers functioned as sitting rooms, workspaces for women, and, when a resident was ill, a place for friends to visit. Access was generally granted to important guests and close family friends; however, there were occasions when bedrooms were opened during larger entertainments.

Sparsely furnished today, during the Aikens' tenure both of the second-floor bedchambers were lavishly decorated with rich textiles and the best of furnishings. Closely following fashion trends, Governor Aiken and his wife purchased impressive *en suite* furniture from the major style centers, most notably New York. The couple owned at least two sets of bedroom furnishings in the popular Greek Revival style. The west bedchamber and its adjacent dressing room contain one such suite, which includes a wardrobe, washstand, dressing bureau, and bed. Featuring clean lines and classical architectural details such as columnar supports and cornice moldings, antebellum tastemakers deemed Greek Revival furniture most appropriate for Italianate mansions or villas such as the Aikens'.

Across the hall in the east bedchamber, a mahogany-veneered bedstead was once a part of a larger bedroom suite. In the French taste, this plain, classically inspired bed was *au courant* and considered modern. American architect and tastemaker Alexander Jackson Downing commented that while the four-poster bedstead remained popular in England, it "is almost entirely laid aside in the United States for the French bedstead, low, and without curtains."[50] The maker of the Aikens' furniture is unknown, but labeled objects still in the possession of descendants and comparative studies suggest that they patronized notable New York cabinetmakers Duncan Phyfe and Deming & Bulkley, the latter of which operated a retail location on King Street in Charleston.

West bedchamber.

Exhibited in the bedroom with the impressive *en suite* Greek Revival furnishings are rare nineteenth-century grass mats. The mats are part of a larger collection from the Aiken-Rhett House and were installed in place of heavier carpeting during the hot summer months. The floor matting was purchased in strips, sewn together lengthwise, and then tacked to the floor, creating a decorative wall-to-wall covering. The folding chair was made by P.J. Hardy and Company and was among the Aiken-Rhett family's later purchases in the 1870s.

East bedchamber.

Made by Deming and Bulkley, the mahogany dressing bureau retains its original maker's label. The New York firm opened its Charleston retail location circa 1820 on King Street, and for the next twenty years, it supplied wealthy Charlestonians, such as the Aikens, with sophisticated furniture as well as a wide variety of domestic goods, including draperies and floor matting. The portraits on the mantel of Andrew Burnet Rhett Jr. and his brother Edmund Rhett are hand-colored image enlargements taken from smaller photographs.

The Dressing Rooms

During the nineteenth century, there was an increasing emphasis on personal cleanliness and a resulting appreciation of privacy. The dressing rooms adjacent to each bedroom were important features of such refined living. However, like bedchambers during the period, the dressing room was not truly a private space. Furniture forms related to grooming were ubiquitous in the houses of well-mannered, genteel families such as the Aikens, but a nineteenth-century dressing room contained other types of furniture as well, often including seating furniture, both chairs and sofas, dressing chests, tables, washstands, and wardrobes.

Dressing rooms in nineteenth-century houses such as the Aiken-Rhett House also served as the primary place to bathe. In a time when water was heated by fire, bathing was not simple. This was obviously considered during the 1858 renovations when a servants' call bell, which is one of many on the site, was installed in the dressing room.

House slaves, unlike their plantation counterparts, had no set working hours. Most of the slaves' duties revolved around the physical care and convenience of their owners, meaning they worked at all hours. Duties associated with the dressing room would have included preparation of baths, emptying chamber pots, and tending the fire.

Although its billowing fabric is now long gone, the table exhibited in the east dressing room reveals its unpainted wood top and wire frame. In the Aiken family's time, however, it would have been dressed with a gathered canopy, table cover, and floor-length skirt, most probably of white fabric and lace like the examples illustrated in Henry Williams's *Beautiful Homes.* Describing the wedding of Henrietta Aiken to Andrew B. Rhett at the Aikens' mountain house in Flat Rock, North Carolina, Mary Boykin Chesnut depicted a chaotic scene that involved a dressing table similar to the one currently in the collection:

Right: **A lady's dressing table.**
The amount of fabric that covered this style of dressing table is illustrated in Henry Williams's 1878 *Beautiful Homes. Courtesy of the Athenaeum of Philadelphia.*

Far right: DRESSING TABLE WITH WROUGHT-IRON DRAPERY FRAME, **circa 1850. Lent by Mary M. Scarborough, L.96.10.9.**

The cloth-covered dressing table was a popular form that came into fashion in the late eighteenth century and was found in Southern houses well into the late nineteenth century. In the Aiken family's time, this table would have been dressed with a gathered canopy, table cover, and floor-length skirt, most probably of white fabric and lace.

The night of the wedding, it stormed as if the world was coming to an end. She [Henrietta] had a Duchess dressing table trimmed with muslin and lace; not one of the shifts of poverty, but a millionaire's attempt at being economical. A candle was left too near this light drapery and it took fire. Outside lightning to fire the world; inside, the bridal chamber ablaze! And enough wind to blow the house down the mountainside. The English maid behaved heroically, and with the aid of Mrs. Aiken and Mrs. Singleton's servants, put out the fire without disturbing the marriage ceremony which was then being performed below. Everything in the bridal chamber was burnt up except the bed, and that was a mass of cinders and smut-flakes of charred and blackened wood. Mrs. Singleton said: "Burnet Rhett has strong nerves, and the bride is too good to be superstitious."[51]

East dressing room.

Dressing rooms were used for bathing. Running water, fed via an attic cistern, was available at the Aiken–Rhett House as early as the 1830s. In the foreground of the photograph is a nineteenth-century baby bath.

The Drawing Room

Constructed as part of the 1830s expansion of the house, the drawing room was built above the second-floor dining room. Perhaps more than any other room in the Aiken-Rhett House, the drawing room contains the best-preserved nineteenth-century decorative elements. When Frances Dill Rhett invited The Charleston Museum's curator, J. Kenneth Jones, into the house for the first time in the spring of 1975, he was particularly struck by this room. He wrote:

The only room the vandals had not penetrated was the massive east bedroom above the dining room…formerly rich wallpaper and borders still decorated the walls. And two most beautiful mirrors in the house faced each other from above the fireplace and on the opposite wall…At the far corner stood a huge sleigh bed, its canopy frame still attached to the ceiling. We couldn't easily examine this room except for a few feet inside the door, as the floor was literally covered with stacks of furniture, trunks, boxes of books and papers. For at least forty years this room had served as a warehouse for numerous family members.[52]

The once grand room in which the Aikens' had entertained their guests had been converted into a bedroom and then a storage room.

One octagonal and two demi-lune ottomans, with fragments of their nineteenth-century upholstery, are exhibited in the room. In 1850, tastemaker A.J. Downing explained, "The *ottoman* is a piece of furniture which we borrow from oriental countries, and which has become quite popular among us of late. It is in excellent keeping with buildings in the classical or Venetian style, and in hot climates, affords a more agreeable lounge than any other seat whatever—while, if made of good breadth, it will also serve as a bed, should occasion require."[53] The demi-lune shaped examples, which could be positioned back to back or singularly, are *en suite* with the sofa in the west parlor and several other banquettes exhibited throughout the house.

Discussion of the drawing room invariably turns to its elaborate and elegant plasterwork. The impressive cast-plaster medallion decorated with acanthus leaves features a large iron hook from which an oil or candle chandelier once hung. Some of Hurricane Hugo's impact on

DETAIL OF HARP, **New York, circa 1820–30, manufactured by J.F. Brown and Co. Gift to Historic Charleston Foundation through transfer from The Charleston Museum, 96.3.76.**

For young women of the antebellum period such as Henrietta Aiken, music was an important part of their education. Harps were considered a genteel instrument suitable for parlor music. The detailing of this harp includes gilded figures standing under Gothic architectural details.

Drawing room.

The drawing room's plaster cornice with leaf-and-vine decoration, central rococo revival ceiling medallion, and ornate wallpaper panels were added during the Aikens' 1858 renovation. These decorative additions likely signaled a change in use from a drawing room to a more formal second-floor parlor. The flocked paper, once a brilliant red, is outlined in a complex overlaid border that imitates molding. This wallpaper was indeed purchased and applied at great expense to the Aikens. The remaining panel fragments, some largely intact, are rare survivals and help us document antebellum decorative treatments.

the house is evident on the upper north wall and ceiling where the rather complex plaster cornice suffered water damage. The cornice design is composed of organic vines and leaves set above a cove. Originally gilded, the coved section of the cornice was painted oxblood red.

The African American Experience at the Aiken-Rhett House

Before the end of the Civil War, William Aiken Jr. was one of the largest slave owners and among the wealthiest men in the United States. His wealth was principally derived from the labor of almost eight hundred enslaved men, women, and children working on Aiken's rice plantation, Jehossee. Located between Charleston and Savannah near Edisto Island, Jehossee is an island of approximately 3,300 acres—1,500 of which were planted in rice and other crops.

Documents from the 1840s and later offer glimpses into the lives of the enslaved African Americans who populated the Aikens' town and country properties. In 1843, the Virginia agriculturalist Edmund Ruffin visited Jehossee and wrote a detailed description of the slave community that labored in the Aiken rice fields:

But a more interesting sight was the negro houses, which in number may be considered as a large village, & certainly the most regular & handsome village of its size that I have seen. For all villages, & even towns, though they may have some splendid edifices, have also many more that are mean, wretched, & offensive to the eye. In this negro village, while every building is plain & humble, every one is also neat, comfortable & pleasing to the view, & still more to the imagination. The houses are of uniform size & construction, (except the church) & are all neatly built of frame-work, & each containing two tenements, & having a brick chimney in the middle. They are all white-washed; & as seen when approaching the plantation, appear to stretch continuously for nearly a mile. In fact the village must be more than half a mile long, besides a vacant interval along the wide

Jehossee oak allée.

Jehossee Plantation was Governor William Aiken Jr.'s main working plantation. Several allées of live oaks survive; however, buildings on the property do not.

Slave quarters ruins, Jehossee Plantation.
By the 1940s, when this photograph was taken, the slave quarters referred to in Edward Ruffin's description of Jehossee Plantation were already in ruins. These chimneys were originally in the center of each building and had two hearths. Known as the saddlebag design, each of the two rooms in the quarters had its own fireplace for warmth and cooking. *Photograph courtesy of Mr. and Mrs. Henry C. Hutson.*

bank which forms part of the road. In the first part of the village there are four rows of houses. Across the causeway three rows, & at the farther extremity two rows. Each house has attached its garden ground, of uniform size, & well enclosed by stake poles. The negroes residing in them are about 700 in number.[54]

Absent from Ruffin's description is any sense of the hard labor and miserable environmental conditions endured by enslaved laborers on a Lowcountry rice plantation. Also absent is any sense of how the slave community at Jehossee might compare to the urban domestic slave community at the Aiken-Rhett House. Several documentary sources and surviving architectural evidence, namely the dependencies and yard of the Aiken-Rhett House, best reveal the daily life of the enslaved individuals at the house.

During the antebellum period, the number of slaves who worked on the property varied from ten to twenty. In 1846, a census survey listed seven adult slaves and their six children living at the Aiken-Rhett House. Ann Greggs and Dorcas Richardson lived here; it is very possible that one or both of these women served as the Aikens' cook. Slaves provided the services and labor that allowed wealthy Charlestonians like the Aikens to live an aristocratic lifestyle similar to that of British gentry. However, this resulted in the loss of the most basic freedom for more than half of Charleston's population.

In 1845, William Aiken became the trustee for stock and slaves belonging to his wife, Harriet. Listed in the trusteeship document were twenty slaves identified by their first names.[55] While most of those individuals remain anonymous, it is possible to identify—at least tentatively—some of them from later accounts. The 1850 federal census listed William Aiken as head of a Charleston County household that included his wife Harriet and daughter Henrietta, as well as a twenty-year-old French woman named Pauline Boudet.[56] The South Carolina slave schedule for 1850 indicated that William Aiken had seven slaves in Charleston County—three male and four female—ranging in age from eighteen to sixty-five.[57] Most likely all seven resided at the Aiken-Rhett House, and it seems likely that the census did not include children under eighteen or slaves older than sixty-five, suggesting a slave community of a dozen or more. City health department records for the 1850s documented the deaths of two domestic slaves from the Aiken-Rhett household—Hetty of hepatitis in 1854 at the age of twenty-three and Phillis of consumption in 1858 at the age of sixteen.[58] Nine years later, the Charleston tax list for 1859 assessed Aiken thirty-six dollars for twelve slaves, while the federal census of 1860 listed William Aiken, his wife and daughter, and nineteen slaves—eight male and eleven female, of which eleven were listed as mulatto, ranging in age from eight to fifty years of age.[59]

The most useful record of slaves at the Aiken-Rhett House is a legal document filed by William Aiken in July 1874. At the time of the Emancipation Proclamation in 1863, Aiken claimed to have fourteen slaves in his "immediate household and in and about his family." They included Tom and Ann Greggs and her son Henry Greggs; Sambo and his wife Dorcas Richardson and her children Charles, Rachael, Victoria, Elizabeth, and Julia; Charles Jackson and Anthony Barnwell; and two carpenters, Will and Jacob.[60]

The 1874 document is the first to identify enslaved family groupings at the Aiken-Rhett House and allows for a comparison with the earlier, less detailed list of Harriet Aiken's slaves in 1845. Tom, Ann, and Henry Greggs appeared on both lists, as did Sambo, Dorcas, and as many as three of their children—Rachael, Victoria, and Elizabeth. Harriet Aiken's slave Phillis died in 1858 and, if the carpenter Will listed for 1863 was the same William who appeared on the 1845 list, then ten of the twenty slaves from that list can be accounted for in the Aiken household almost two decades later.

The working-age slaves performed a wide array of functions in the Aiken household—cooking, laundry, and cleaning, as well as gardening, caring for horses in the stable, and driving the family coach. All lived in the second-story quarters of the two brick dependencies. As first constructed by John Robinson in 1820s, the kitchen dependency had two bedchambers on the second story, but Aiken's expansion of the building in the 1830s added three more bedchambers upstairs, a first-floor room that is believed to have served as a second kitchen dedicated to the slave household, and two second-story bedchambers for the stable hands in the stable/carriage house.

If the 1863 enumeration of slaves is accurate and complete, then it is possible to speculate to some extent on their distribution within the two dependencies and also their duties and skills. It seems likely that the Greggs and Richardson families would have occupied the rooms in the east or kitchen dependency, while the four single men (Jackson, Barnwell, and the two carpenters) would have shared the two bedchambers over the carriage house. Cooking and domestic housekeeping would have been conducted by Ann Greggs, Dorcas Richardson, and the Richardson daughters, while other duties would have been shared by Tom Greggs, Sambo Richardson, Charles Jackson, and Anthony Barnwell. The carpenters Will and Jacob most likely were hired out as skilled laborers to work elsewhere in the city. While this evaluation is highly speculative, the Aiken slave enumeration of 1863 combined with an undisturbed slave environment provides one of the most complete records of an urban slave community in Charleston, and also the South.[61]

Rice harvest at Jehossee.

An 1866 Freedmen's Bureau document lists former slave Simon Boggs as the recipient of a forty-acre land grant on Governor Aiken's Jehossee Plantation. Boggs family members continued to live on the plantation well into the twentieth century. William Boggs was photographed in the 1940s during one of the last rice harvests on Jehossee. *Photograph courtesy of Mr. and Mrs. Henry C. Hutson.*

Slave quarter and east dependency.

Measuring twelve and a half feet by fifteen feet, this room was painted red during the early twentieth century. Unfortunately, inventories of Aiken family possessions did not list items owned by the house slaves. However, each room most likely had a bed, table, and some form of seating.

Warming Kitchen and Servants' Hall

The warming kitchen, located in the basement of the house, was part of the service area primarily used by enslaved African Americans. Most cooking took place in the dependency building behind the main house. Slaves used the warming kitchen to garnish and ready foods for presentation in the formal dining room directly above them. The "back stairs" just outside the room allowed access to the dining room. The stairs signify the melding of the enslaved and free worlds, as the servants used the steps to access the formal entertaining rooms of the house.

Today the warming kitchen is furnished similarly to how it would have been during the antebellum period, with wire-covered pie safes, storage cabinets, and plate warmers. The kitchen room, like many others in the Aiken-Rhett House, contains a variety of lighting fixtures. A metal gas fixture is located in the center of the room above the pine table. The remnants of an early knob-and-tube electrical wiring system installed in the early part of the twentieth century can be seen on the ceiling. The warming kitchen is an example of Historic Charleston Foundation's preservation policy: all layers of the house's history are preserved.

Warming kitchen.

Added during the 1835 expansion, what has been interpreted as a warming kitchen could have been a servants' gathering space as well as a place in which final preparations were made to food before its presentation in the dining room directly above. Despite its role as a utilitarian space, the room's floor is imported flagstone; the mantelpiece—perhaps recycled from an upper-story room—is purely decorative; and the installation of gas lighting during the 1850s is visible.

East and West Dependency

The building that houses the Aikens' kitchen and slave quarters compares closely in design and style to Charleston's other nineteenth-century urban dependencies. It was a two-story structure, with two rooms flanking a central passage and with corresponding quarters for slaves upstairs that were accessed by an indoor staircase. Outside, the walls were laid in Flemish bond using the same type of Savannah gray bricks found on the main house and finished with a traditional Charleston "beak" joint that was tuck-pointed with a bright white lime mortar.

The placement of the kitchen in a separate building was intentional in the antebellum South. The threat of fire and the often-under-mentioned smells that must have come from food preparation

Slave quarters hallway.

Perhaps best described as a dormitory configuration, the slave quarters on the second floor of the kitchen building have five rooms.

in an era before consistent refrigeration are the understandable reasons for establishing some distance between kitchen and main house.

Governor Aiken expanded the dependency in the 1830s; the effect was both an enlargement of the original facility and a redecorating of its façades in the Gothic Revival style. The building was extended in length by thirty-five feet and both floors were remodeled to include more convenient workspaces and additional quarters on the upper floor.

Over the course of the nineteenth century, changes were made to the interior of the kitchen portion. Most notable was the installation of the cooking range, or "stew stove," after the Civil War. Directly in front of the range is a stone hearth, installed to prevent stray embers from igniting a fire. There is a remarkable array of kitchen furnishings that survive in the kitchen, including storage cabinets, a pie safe, and a small metal-lined chest that was used to store ice.

The second floor contains a series of dormitory-style rooms, which were the setting for slave family life. Each was simply furnished with beds, tables, chairs, and the slaves' personal possessions. Many of these rooms also contain pegboards that were used for hanging clothing. The interior windows in the hallway furnished light and minimal air ventilation. With one exception, each room contained a fireplace, although not all of the fireplaces remain intact.

In comparison to the quarters of their plantation counterparts, it is generally accepted that conditions of urban slave quarters varied by the slave's occupation, reflecting a hierarchy where house servants had the most prestigious quarters, living in rooms such as the ones at the Aiken–Rhett House.

Kitchen.

As evidenced here, nineteenth-century kitchens throughout the South were most often housed in separate buildings. The perception that slave spaces were always whitewashed certainly does not hold true at the Aiken-Rhett House. Visible evidence of the paint history in this building indicates that over time the walls were brightly painted in yellows, pinks, reds, and oranges.

The backyard overview.

Archaeological investigation indicates that the back lot included six extant outbuildings as well as an ornamental garden with a magnolia allée in the center of the lot. Only three of the magnolia trees remain. The stables and carriage house on the left were doubled in size by Governor Aiken at the same time as the kitchen and main slave quarters on the right. During the renovation, Gothic Revival window casements were added and the exterior was lime washed yellow to match the main house.

Excavation of the yard, showing archaeologist Martha Zierden at work.

The Charleston Museum, under Zierden's direction, has supervised two excavations at the Aiken–Rhett House. Analysis of pollen collected from dirt samples taken during the digs revealed that numerous exotic and native species of decorative plants were grown by the Aikens. Other artifacts from the digs included butchered animal bones, shards of china, and a previously unknown well. *Photograph from the archives of Historic Charleston Foundation.*

Stables and Carriage House

Stables.

This Historic American Buildings Survey photograph by Charles N. Bayless documents the condition of the stables in 1979. The Gothic-style arches were part of the 1830s renovations, during which the building was roughly doubled in size, bringing the total number of horse stalls to six. Vertical openings along the outside wall allow for air circulation.

The stables contained six stalls that were highly finished with decorative columns and gothic arches. The level of detail in the architectural facets suggests that the stable was intended to be viewed by guests and that Aiken greatly prized his horses. Of note are openings in the exterior walls for air circulation, a feature missing in the slave quarters.

Tack was hung on a line of pegs and stored close to the stalls. A narrow staircase leads to the hayloft, where a large pulley on a swing arm was used to haul bales of hay into the storage space. The hay was dropped through shoots in the floor to the mangers mounted to the walls of the stalls below. Also on the second floor were two rooms for the enslaved African American grooms or hostlers. Despite their proximity to the flammable hay loft, both of the rooms have fireplaces.

Two carriages that belonged to the Aikens are still in the carriage house portion of the building. One is a cabriolet built around 1870 and the other is a landaulet, circa 1880. Landaulets were typically used for making social calls and city traveling.

The Yard

The Aiken–Rhett House is one of America's few urban town houses where outbuildings have remained largely unchanged since the nineteenth century. Although fragile, this portion of the complex is so remarkably intact that it represents one of the most complete urban dependency groups with early fittings to survive anywhere in the South. Work yards, varying in size and complexity, were part of almost every Charleston town house property in the first half of the nineteenth century and were the domain of slaves.

The back lot boasted an ornamental garden, an allée of trees, two privies, and two additional structures along the east and west walls that were possibly follies. Evidence also shows that an avenue of Southern magnolia, several of which were destroyed by Hurricane Gracie in 1959, filled the center of the lot. Originally, there were at least five trees on each side leading from the back gate to the carriage house.

Even after the completion of an archaeological survey, the history of the back lot is not fully understood. During Aiken's time, four smaller buildings, three of which remain today, stood to the north of the large east and west dependencies. The two back corner buildings have been identified as privies, but the function of the others remains inconclusive. Based on their construction and Gothic Revival architectural detailing, these structures are thought to be part of Governor Aiken's 1835 or 1858 improvements to the property.

View of the privy.
The level of decorative detail in the masonry and architectural detail of the Gothic Revival–style structures in the back lot belie their role as support structures.

CONCLUSION

The Nathaniel Russell House embodies many of the grandest architectural and decorative elements available to craftsmen in the early nineteenth century, making it stand out as one of the great neoclassical houses in America. From the intricate woodwork to the use of ornamental plaster and ironwork, the Russell House was designed to display an exuberance and celebration of wealth during Charleston's most prosperous era. The extensive use of gold leaf and rare pigments coupled with the spectacular artistry shown in the trompe l'oeil cornices and faux-grained mahogany doors indicate an almost ostentatious display of embellishment. The free-flying or cantilevered staircase shows a desire to push the limits of engineering and construction to create yet another feature that distinguished this grand house from the others. The complexity of the Russell House is reinforced even in subtle ways through the use of geometry in designing rooms that are square, rectangular, and oval on each floor. The house serves as a study of refinement and prosperity in early nineteenth-century America and is a treasure for those who want to experience Federal architecture at its finest.

The intrigue surrounding the Aiken-Rhett House revolves around its distinctive and mostly intact architectural evolution. Its unrestored interior and outbuildings clearly give today's visitors a glimpse of the grandeur and lifestyle of a wealthy Charleston family that lived on the property for more than a century and a half. The architectural distinction of the house's original late Federal style, with its significant Greek Revival and Victorian modifications, can be studied like a textbook. The collection of intact outbuildings provides an unparalleled understanding of the working side of an urban town house in the antebellum South. Almost without exception, visitors find the Aiken-Rhett House the most interesting and enlightening historic house museum in Charleston. Its clear evolution of styles and its unrestored interior make it a rare find for those interested in the details and nuances of architecture not normally evident in a restored house.

Glenn F. Keyes, AIA
PRESERVATION ARCHITECT
2008

NOTES

The Nathaniel Russell House

1. Nathaniel Russell, Charleston, to the Reverend Ezra Stiles, Newport, RI, July 19, 1767, published in Orlando Ridout and Willie William Graham, eds., *An Architectural and Historical Analysis of the Nathaniel Russell House Charleston, South Carolina,* vol. IIIa (Historic Charleston Foundation, 1995).

2. See advertisements: *South Carolina Gazette*, May 18, 1769; *South Carolina Gazette and General Advertiser*, June 13, 1785; *South Carolina Weekly Gazette*, June 18–22, 1785.

3. *South Carolina Gazette and General Advertiser*, June 13, 1785; Nathaniel Russell, Charleston, to Aaron Lopez, Newport, RI, November 27, 1773, in *An Architectural and Historical Analysis*, vol. IIIa.

4. Martha A. Zierden, "Archaeological Contributions 24," *Initial Archeological Testing: The Nathaniel Russell House* (unpub. ms. for Historic Charleston Foundation, March 1995), 16; *Charleston Courier*, June 9, 1804.

5. *Charleston Courier*, May 10, 1808.

6. *Charleston Courier*, September 11, 1811; *The Times*, September 17, 1811.

7. "Last Will and Testament of Nathaniel Russell," Wills of Charleston County, 1671-1868, Book F 1818–1826, 157. South Carolina Room, Charleston County Public Library.

8. Abiel Abbot, *A Journal of a Voyage to South Carolina*, unpub. ms. (1818), 39. Abbot Family Papers, South Carolina Historical Society.

9. Nathaniel Bowen, Providence, RI, to Susan Bowen, Boston, August 4, 1802. Bowen-Cooke Papers, South Carolina Historical Society.

10. Margaret Izard Manigault, Charleston, to Mary Stead Pinckney, Pinckney's Island, SC, Manigault Papers, South Caroliniana Library.

11. Margaret Izard Manigault, Charleston, to Alice Delancey Izard, Philadelphia, Izard Papers, Library of Congress.

12. Catherine Van Horne Read, Charleston, to Elizabeth Van Horne Ludlow, New York, July 21, 1813. Read Family Papers, South Caroliniana Library, University of South Carolina.

13. *Charleston Courier*, April 12, 1820.

14. Henry D. Lesesne to Adele Petigru Allston, Summerville, June 18, 1857, *The South Carolina Rice Plantation as Revealed in the Papers of Robert F.W. Allston*, ed. Harold Easterby (Chicago: University of Chicago Press, 1945), 138.

15. John Oliver Killens, ed. *The Trial Record of Denmark Vesey* (Boston: Beacon Press, 1970) 81–82.

16. Walter Edgar, ed. *The South Carolina Encyclopedia* (Columbia: The University of South Carolina Press, 2006), 19.

17. See Getty Project Implementation Grant Proposal, Historic Charleston Foundation Curatorial Files.

18. Elizabeth W. Allston Pringle, *Chronicles of Chicora Wood* (Boston: Christopher Publishing House, 1940), 191.

19. Ibid., 169–71.

20. For more information see Zierden, "Archaeological Contributions 24," *Initial Archeological Testing*, 25.

21. Pringle, *Chicora Wood*, 307.

22. See *Report of Committee on Condition of Buildings after the Earthquake, with a List of Buildings that Should Come Down*, South Carolina Room, Charleston County Public Library.

23. HCF Minutes, March 8, 1948.

24. Robert Weyeneth, *Historic Preservation for a Living City: Historic Charleston Foundation 1947-1997* (Columbia: University of South Carolina Press, 2000), 54.

25. The desk without its bookcase is illustrated in Susan Pringle Frost's *Highlights of the Miles Brewton House* (1944). It was located on the first floor of the south parlor. Bradford L. Rauschenberg and John Bivins Jr., vol. II (Winston-Salem: Museum of Early Southern Decorative Arts, 2003), 464. Museum Department, Object File, Memo from Jonathan Poston to Russell House docents, April 19, 2000.

26. Maurie D. McInnis, *The Politics and Taste in Antebellum Charleston* (Chapel Hill: University of North Carolina, 2005), 287.

27. Pringle, *Chicora Wood*, 187.

The Aiken-Rhett House

28. *Charleston Courier*, September 21, 1825.

29. *Charleston Courier*, July 12, 1827.

30. The date of the Aikens' move into the renovated house is based on listings in the Charleston City Directories for the Years 1835 and 1836.

31. From a letter written to Francis Kinloch Middleton, February 24, 1839. Cheves-Middleton Papers, the South Carolina Historical Society.

32. Andrew B. Rhett to Henrietta Aiken, n.d. Aiken-Rhett Collection, The Charleston Museum, Charleston, South Carolina.

33. Ben Ames Williams, ed., *A Diary from Dixie, Mary Boykin Chesnut* (Cambridge, MA: Harvard University Press, 1998), 276–77.

34. Andrew B. Rhett to Edmund Rhett, August 10, 1862. Private collection. Copy available in Aiken-Rhett Family Research, Andrew B. Rhett Correspondence file, Museum Department, Historic Charleston Foundation.

35. Ibid.; *A Diary from Dixie,* 306–07.

36. *New York Times*, May 14, 1865, 2.
37. *New York Times*, August 8, 1863, 5. See Elizabeth W. Garrett, "Entertainment of the Most Beautiful Kind: The House of William Aiken and Harriet Aiken, 1833–1860" (master's thesis, University of Delaware, 2005), 4–5.
38. Invoices dated December 1874, Box 41, Aiken-Rhett Collection, The Charleston Museum, Charleston, South Carolina.
39. William Aiken to Joseph Daniel Aiken, December 11, 1885. Aiken-Rhett Collection, The Charleston Museum, Charleston, South Carolina.
40. *Charleston News and Courier*, September 8, 1887.
41. Invoice to Henrietta Aiken Rhett from A. O'Connell, Painter and Dealer in Paints, Oils, Glass, Etc., 84 Meeting Street, August 8, 1891. Aiken-Rhett Collection, The Charleston Museum, Charleston, South Carolina.
42. Henrietta Aiken Rhett to Edmund Rhett, n.d. Box 7, letters 1870s to 1932, Aiken-Rhett Collection, The Charleston Museum, Charleston, South Carolina.
43. "Aunt Elise" of Waverly Place, Schenectady, New York, to Burnet Rhett, February 6, 1925. Box 7, Aiken-Rhett Collection, The Charleston Museum, Charleston, South Carolina. "Aiken" presumably refers to William Aiken Rhett, Burnet's older brother.
44. Frederika Bremer, *The Homes of the New World; Impressions of America*, translated by Mary Howitt, vol. 1 (New York: Harper & Brothers, 1858), 389.
45. Mary Huger Cottenet to Harriet Lowndes Aiken. Aiken-Rhett Collection, The Charleston Museum, Charleston, South Carolina.
46. Ben Ames Williams, ed., *A Diary from Dixie, Mary Boykin Chesnut* (Cambridge, MA: Harvard University Press, 1998), 322.
47. See Nathaniel Bishop. *Voyage of the Paper Canoe* (New York: Lee Shepard, 1878).
48. Travel Diary of Harriet Lowndes Aiken, 1857-58, Box 73, Aiken-Rhett Collection, The Charleston Museum, Charleston, South Carolina.
49. Copy of the article credited to Eola Willis, n.d. Archives of Historic Charleston Foundation.
50. A.J. Downing, *The Architecture of Country Houses* (1850; reprint, with an introduction by J. Stewart Johnson, New York: Dover Publications, 1969), 431.
51. Williams, *Diary from Dixie*, 306–07.
52. J. Kenneth Jones, "Spring 1975, The Aiken Rhett House, The First Visit" (paper written for The Charleston Museum, July 21, 1989). Historic Charleston Foundation Curatorial Files.
53. Downing, *Architecture of Country Houses*, 427.
54. See *Agriculture, Geology, and Society in Antebellum South Carolina: The Private Diary of Edmund Ruffin, 1843* (Athens: University of Georgia Press, 1992). Similar descriptions of Jehossee are published in the *Charleston Courier* on July 18, 1844, and in J.D.B. De Bow, *The Industrial Resources, Statistics, Etc. of the United States, and more Particularly the Southern and*

Western States, Vol. II (New York: D. Appleton & Company, 1854), 424–25. The latter source notes, "Nearly all the land has been reclaimed, and the buildings, except the [owner's] house, erected new, within the twenty years that Governor Aiken has owned the island." Aiken did not own the entire island at this time, but acquired an additional twelve hundred acres in 1859. See Colleton County RMC, Deed Book F-14, 204.

55. Charleston County Deed Book R-11, 522. The slaves named are Ann, Kelly, Thomas, Phoebe, Ann, Elizabeth, Henry, Sambo, Dorcas, Phillis, Rachael, Victoria, Eliza, Betsey, Elijah, William, Dinah, Judy, Andrew and Molly.

56. United States Census for South Carolina, 1850.

57. South Carolina Slave Schedule, 1850, Charleston County Public Library.

58. Charleston Health Department Records, January 1853 to December 1857 and December 1857 to December 1859, Charleston County Public Library.

59. *List of the Tax Payers of the City of Charleston for 1859*, Charleston County Public Library.

60. U.S. District Court document. Box 1, Aiken-Rhett Collection, The Charleston Museum, Charleston, South Carolina.

61. In February 1863, the deaths of two more Aiken slaves were recorded: Lizzie died of consumption at the age of thirty and William died of typhoid/pneumonia at age fourteen. See Charleston Health Department Records, January 1863–December 1865, Charleston County Public Library.